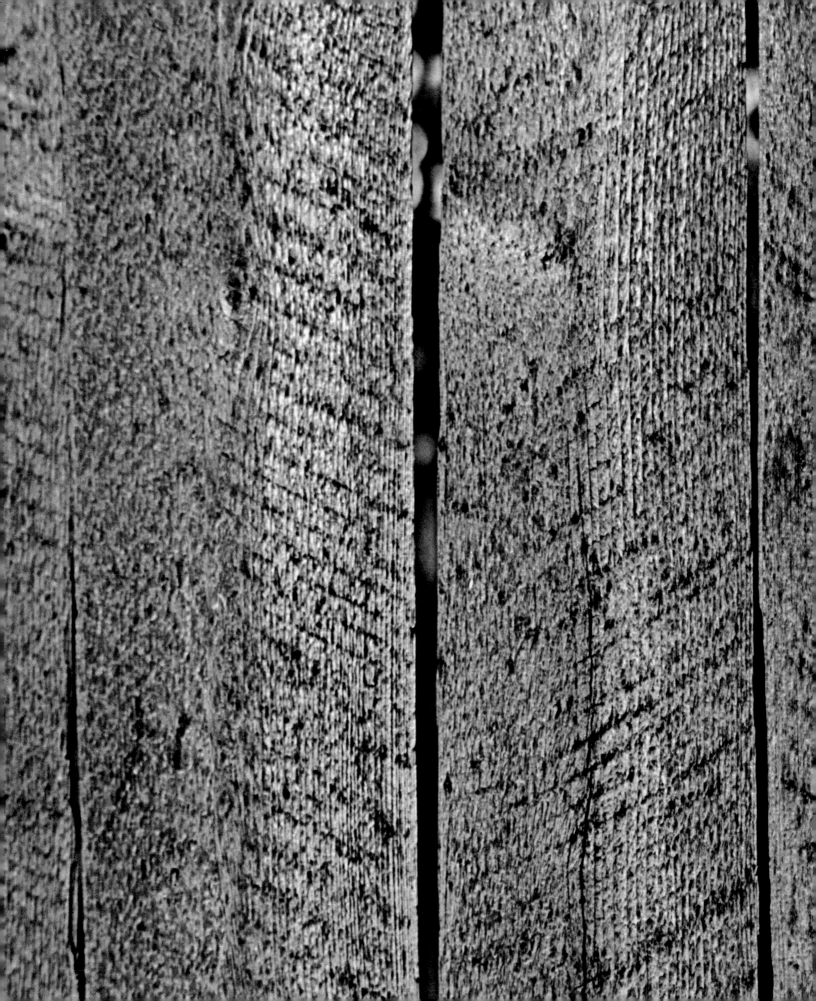

THE FAMILY CREATIVE WORKSHOP

15

Rosemaling, Rubbings
Rya and Flossa, Sail Making and Repair
Samplers, Sandal Making
Sand Casting, Sand Characters and Castles
Sand Painting and Layering
Sashimi and Sushi, Scrimshaw

Plenary Publications International, Inc.
New York and Amsterdam

Published by Plenary Publications International, Incorporated 300 East 40 Street, New York, N. Y. 10016, for the Blue Mountain Crafts Council

Library of Congress Catalog Card Number: 73-89331.
Complete set International Standard Book Number: 0-88459-021-6
Volume 15 International Standard Book Number: 0-88459-014-3

Manufactured in the United States of America. Printed and bound by the W. A. Krueger Company, Brookfield, Wisconsin.

Printing preparation by Lanman Lithoplate Company.

Publishers:

Plenary Publications International, Incorporated
300 East 40 Street
New York, New York 10016

Steven R. Schepp
EDITOR

Jerry Curcio
PRODUCTION MANAGER

Editorial preparation:

Tree Communications, Inc.
250 Park Avenue South
New York, New York 10003

Rodney Friedman
EDITORIAL DIRECTOR

Ronald Gross
DESIGN DIRECTOR

Paul Levin
DIRECTOR OF PHOTOGRAPHY

Jill Munves
TEXT EDITOR

Sonja Douglas
ART DIRECTOR

Rochelle Lapidus
Marsha Gold
DESIGNERS

Lucille O'Brien
EDITORIAL PRODUCTION

Ruth Forst Michel
COPYREADER

Eva Gold
ADMINISTRATIVE MANAGER

Editors for this volume:

Andrea DiNoto
SCRIMSHAW

Donal Dinwiddie
SAIL MAKING AND REPAIR

Michael Donner
SAND PAINTING AND LAYERING

Linda Hetzer
SANDAL MAKING
SAND CASTING

Nancy Bruning Levine
RYA AND FLOSSA
SASHIMI AND SUSHI

Marilyn Nierenberg
RUBBINGS
SAND CHARACTERS AND CASTLES

Mary Grace Skurka
ROSEMALING
SAMPLERS

Originating editor of the series:
Allen Davenport Bragdon

Contributing editor:
Alice Richard

Contributing illustrators:
Marina Givotovsky
Lynn Matus
Marilyn Nierenberg
Sally Shimizu

Contributing photographers:
Steven Mays
Marilyn Nierenberg
Judy Thom

Production:

Thom Augusta
Christopher Jones
Patricia Lee
Leslie Strong

The Project-Evaluation Symbols appearing in the title heading at the beginning of each project have these meanings:

Range of approximate cost:

¢ Low: under $5 or free and found natural materials

$ Medium: about $10

$$ High: above $15

Estimated time to completion for an unskilled adult:

Hours

Days

Weeks

Suggested level of experience:

Child alone

Supervised child or family project

Unskilled adult

Specialized prior training

Tools and equipment:

Small hand tools

Large hand and household tools

Specialized or powered equipment

On the cover:
In this detail of a sand-layered scene by Philip Perl, wispy pink clouds streak across a coral sunset sky over the calm blue waters of a mountain lake. See "Sand Painting and Layering," beginning on page 1888. Photograph by Paul Levin.

**Contents and
craftspeople for Volume 15:**

ROSEMALING
Norwegian Folk Art

LOWER NORWAY

Hallingdal

Atlantic Ocean

Telemark

Rogaland

Sweden

North Sea

Denmark

A
Figure A: A map of lower Norway shows the juxtaposition of the regions of Hallingdal and Telemark, where rosemaling reached its most advanced stage. In nearby Rogaland, a painting style was developed that combined the styles of its two neighbors.

Rosemaling, the style of interior decoration popular in Norway from 1700 to 1850, encompasses a wide variety of floral, leaf, and other motifs painted on smooth, prepainted wooden surfaces. The patterns echo the wood carvings of earlier times; rosemaling may have evolved from the painting of such carvings. In its prime, rosemaling was not limited to small pieces of furniture and utensils as it generally is now. It covered walls, doors, ceilings, built-in cupboards, large dowry chests, and bedsteads of the peasants' rustic log cottages as well. When machine-made things became widely available, rosemaling (as well as many other handcrafts) fell into disuse. Only recently have some Norwegians revived this traditional art, often decorating one room in a home in what is termed country style.

Rose painting, as rosemaling is sometimes called, is kin to Russian decorative painting (though it does not share that country's enthusiasm for gold leaf) and to Pennsylvania Dutch art, which originated in Germany. Neither of these can surpass rosemaling in gaiety and naive beauty. The Norwegian style of painting mixes bold shapes with delicate lines, combines contrasting colors, and often uses a border of color or design to frame the central motif.

The colors, used in varying combinations, are limited: reds, yellows (chiefly yellow ocher), moderate greens, blues, and white (often a soft, old-looking white) for the designs, and dull blues or blue-greens, brick reds or red-oranges for the backgrounds. Black outlines and accents are very important, giving the designs depth and definition. White or a pale yellow is used as highlight or accent color. In antique rosemaling, it is not certain how bright or muted the original colors were and how much time, heat, and fireplace smoke have affected them. The painters did not have varnish; so the rich patina of antique pieces is the result of years of wear.

The Differing Regional Styles

Rosemaling styles developed in several regions of Norway, and at first, each was quite distinct, since mountain ranges separated and isolated these areas. But near the borders, styles overlapped. Itinerant craftsmen (men were the rosemalers), brides with dowry chests who moved away from home, and traveling merchants helped spread the influence of one style or another. The art appeared first in central and southwestern Norway; the districts of Hallingdal and Telemark (see map, left) seem to have had prolific painters who attained a high degree of proficiency. In the nearby area of Rogaland, these two styles were blended to create a third.

The Hallingdal style is easier to execute than the Telemark style. Its colors are bright, with a predominance of red, and the emphasis is on flower forms more than on leaves. The flower shapes are big and important, with scrolls added at the sides merely to suggest leaves. Each half of the design is a mirror image of the other, perfectly balanced, with flat shapes that have little illusion of contour and fewer details than are found in the Telemark designs. Light is assumed to come from above, so all highlighting is applied on the tops of shapes; these light over strokes are not shaded or blended into the adjacent colors. In the projects that follow, the hand mirror (page 1803) and the bread board (page 1805) are painted in this Hallingdal style.

The Telemark style of painting is more complex and more tightly controlled. The design is usually asymmetrical and thick with flowing, elongated scrolls that intertwine. There are many C-shaped and S-shaped curves, rococo leaves and tendrils, and daintily stylized flowers on long, swaying stems. Tonal gradations of color simulate the rounded contours of living plants. Fine decorative accent lines and outlining strokes add depth to both scrolls and flowers. The round plate (page 1808) and treasure box (page 1810) are decorated in the Telemark style.

This rosemaling design, derived from those of the Rogaland region of southern Norway, is typical in that it is a combination of styles that developed in the neighboring Hallingdal and Telemark regions. The mirror-image motif and the naturalistic flower forms are borrowed from Hallingdal, while the graceful scrolls shaded from light to dark and the black accent lines suggest Telemark painting. The combination results in a design that has warmth, gaiety, and charm.

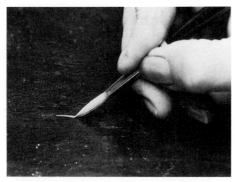

1: Point and pressure are the basic rosemaling brush strokes. To make a point, lightly touch the loaded brush onto the surface and pull it toward you in a thin, even line.

2: For the pressure stroke, continue to pull the brush toward you but at the same time, apply pressure to flatten the brush so it paints a broad line. These steps may be reversed or combined.

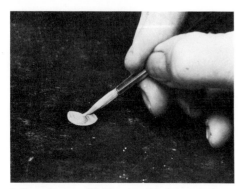

3: To make a small ball, start with the pressure stroke and turn a complete circle with the side of the brush. Do not lift the brush midway. Larger balls can be made with C-shaped filling-in strokes.

The Rogaland style, which evolved from the Hallingdal and Telemark styles, mixes a balanced design and naturalistic flower forms (from the Hallingdal) with scrolls shaded from light to dark and accents of fine contour lines (from the Telemark). The painted design pictured on page 1799 is an example of the Rogaland combination style.

Materials and Tools

Today, rosemaling designs are painted with tube oils on prepainted wood surfaces. If you are working on new wood, prepare it for decorating by giving it two coats of background color, sanding each coat with fine sandpaper. Use a water-based latex enamel and a polyfoam brush that can be rinsed easily. A little paint goes a long way—a half pint will cover a large dowry chest or six small treasure boxes. I custom-mixed the background colors used on the projects that follow; you can make your own by adding universal tinting colors to a basic background paint or approximate the colors with commercial brands. Old wood that is being decorated should be clean and free of all grease or wax. If the old finish is badly marred, strip it off with finish remover and start fresh.

The color palette for rosemaling is uncomplicated. You can mix all the colors you need with these 11 tube oils: Prussian blue; cadmium red light; cadmium yellow light and cadmium yellow deep; yellow ocher; raw umber and burnt umber; raw sienna and burnt sienna; ivory black; and titanium white. Each of the following projects has a color key for mixing the suggested colors from these basic oils.

The tube oils must be broken down with a medium that will speed drying. A good medium can be made with two teaspoons each of mastic varnish, rectified turpentine, and linseed oil, plus a couple of drops of cobalt drier, all available in hardware or art supply stores. Store this mixture in a screw-top jar and pour a small amount as needed into a cup or bottle cap. Tube oil paint mixed with this medium will dry in about four hours. Because varnish is included, none is needed after decorating, but you could protect the design with a semigloss varnish, lightly rubbed down with fine steel wool. Do not use flat varnish; it would cause the painting to lose depth. You will need two brushes, a No. 5 pointed sable watercolor brush and a No. 3 sable scroller. Buy the best brushes you can find; they are worth their cost. Ideally, you would have one brush for each color, but one of each size is enough if you clean both well with deodorized paint thinner between colors.

In addition, you will need: blackboard chalk or graphite transfer paper; tracing paper; a dry ball-point pen or stylus; paper towels for brush wipers; a wooden lath or ruler and two blocks of wood to act as a bridge for your hand to rest on; a paper palette pad or sheets of waxed paper to hold the paints; clear plastic wrap; a palette knife or flat wooden stick for mixing paint colors; a white vinyl eraser; architect's drafting tape; and soft rags.

The Basic Strokes

There are five basic painting strokes in rosemaling: the teardrop; the C-shaped curve which is often used for filling in large areas; the S-shaped curve or scroll; the small ball; and the accent line. All the strokes used to make the basic shapes and those used in the overlays that give contour to flat designs are applications of the first four. Basic shapes and heavier overlays are painted with the watercolor brush. Fine overlays and accent lines are done with the smaller scroller.

It is important to practice all of the strokes before you start a project. Squeeze out a dot of white on your palette and mix in the medium with the palette knife or stick until the paint becomes thin and soft, but not runny, with the consistency of whipped cream. Then wet the watercolor brush with medium, wipe off the excess, and stroke the brush through the paint, loading it evenly up to the metal ferrule. (Always wet the brush with medium before touching the paint.) The paint should move down and off the brush smoothly without dripping. Twirl the brush in the paint to form a point at the tip. Since many strokes begin with a point, remember to repoint your brush each time you load it with paint.

Hold the brush between your thumb and forefinger as you would hold a pencil, steady your hand, and touch the point of the brush to the practice board, a painted piece of cardboard or wood (photograph 1). Next, put pressure on the brush, pull it toward you with your fingers, flatten it to make a broad stroke (photograph 2), and

4: A piece of cardboard or wood painted the background color of your project is a good practice board on which to plan your design colors and practice the strokes you will be using.

lift it off. In rosemaling, you always paint toward yourself. Plant forms other than central flower motifs are painted from the base out, following the direction of natural growth. Turn the piece you are painting in any direction necessary to make these motions possible. Repetition of the point, pressure, and lift, along with strokes of even width, are the basic painting techniques used in rosemaling.

The teardrop can be either point-pressure-lift (the tail on top) or pressure-point-lift (the tail on the bottom). It may swing to the left or the right. A point-pressure-point sequence will give you a leaf shape. The small ball shape is made by painting a complete circle with the side of the brush (photograph 3). Curves used for filling in, scrolls, and contouring overlays are combinations of point-and-pressure strokes with even-width strokes, depending on the length and thickness desired. Usually, it is best to apply overlays while the basic shapes are still wet, so the overlays will blend in at the edges. If you wait until the first layer of paint is dry, the overlay layer will stand out more from the surface and will be less subtle. Some rosemaling painters did this, and you may want to try it at times for a special effect. But remember that each stroke—whether basic, overlay, or accent—must be continuous; you cannot stop and lift the brush midway and still achieve the smooth, fluid curve that is the mark of rosemaling. Fine accent lines that are added on top of and surrounding the basic shapes (*after* that paint is dry) are made with the smaller brush and with paint that is considerably thinner than the basic paint, but the strokes are the same. These lines must be painted slowly with a light touch, so the paint can flow smoothly down the brush into a continuous line. To paint accents and fine overlays, support your hand so that it is directly above the object being painted and you can hold the brush perpendicular to the surface (see photographs 8, 10, and 11, page 1804). When outlining circular tendrils (photograph 10), hold your hand and the brush perfectly still and let wrist action control the curve. This is the one exception to the rule that all strokes are controlled by finger motion.

5: Following the color key given with each project, cluster dots of tube oil paint on your palette and blend them with a palette knife until the desired shade is achieved. As shown, a light brick red is achieved by blending equal parts of cadmium yellow light, cadmium red light, and burnt sienna.

Preparing the Palette

With the 11 tube oils listed on page 1800, you can mix a variety of traditional rosemaling colors. Follow the color keys with each project to mix the colors for that project. In most cases, you use pure ivory black or equal parts of ivory black and raw umber to make the accent and overlay strokes. (Against a dark background, white or pale yellow is sometimes used.) Squeeze out a small dot of each of the colors needed, clustering—but not immediately mixing—those that will be blended together. With the palette knife, separate and mix small amounts of the colors needed in the proportions given. Keep mixing a little at a time until you arrive at the desired color (photograph 5).

Note: Do not use a brush to mix colors except when you want a light blue. Then dip the brush into dark blue, then into medium, then stroke it through white. Do not try to add white to the dark blue to lighten it; it would take too much time and paint. To dull the dark blue, add black; adding raw umber or burnt umber gives the blue a decidedly greenish cast.

To judge the overall color combination, paint a piece of cardboard or wood the background color of your object; then practice the strokes in the colors indicated on that board (photograph 4, page 1801). This way, you can adjust the color proportions before you start to decorate the object, should any changes be necessary.

CRAFTNOTES: TRANSFERRING A DESIGN

A full-sized pattern can be transferred onto the painted object being decorated with either blackboard chalk or graphite transfer paper, depending on the color of the background paint. Use a dry ball-point pen or stylus to trace the pattern. But do not press hard; this would create dents in the wood that you could not hide with paint. Lift a corner of the pattern occasionally to make sure all the lines are being transferred clearly.

With blackboard chalk

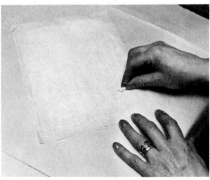

If the background is a deep color, the design must be outlined with white, pale yellow, or some other light color. Trace the pattern onto a sheet of tracing paper; then rub blackboard chalk over the entire back of the paper (above). Do not use pastel chalk; it is too waxy.

Position the tracing paper, chalk side down, on top of the object and tape the corners down with masking tape. Then go over the pattern lines with a dry ball-point pen or a stylus. The chalk outline (above) can be painted over without show-through.

With graphite transfer paper

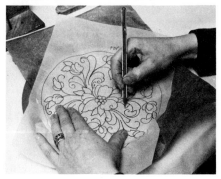

If the background is a light color, the design will be most visible if you place graphite paper, face down, between the tracing and the background (above). Go over the pattern with a dry ball-point pen or a stylus.

The resulting graphite outline (above) should be rubbed lightly with a soft rag until it is barely visible. Otherwise it might show through light-color paints.

Pat Virch's daughter, Julie, can beam with pride because she painted the cheerful flower design on the back of her hand mirror.

Color key

Dark blue	Three parts Prussian blue; one part ivory black; one part titanium white
Dark green	Equal parts of cadmium yellow light; ivory black; and raw umber
Old white	Titanium white with just a bit of raw sienna and raw umber

Basic designs like the Hallingdal flower can be applied to many objects. Here it has been used on a sandwich of matchboxes as well as a hand mirror. To assemble the matchboxes, glue four boxes between two squares of ⅛-inch-thick plywood, after a design has been painted on the top square. Variations in detail make each piece unique, a mark of handcrafting.

Designs and Decorations
Julie's hand mirror

My daughter, Julie, is learning the art of rosemaling by doing—she painted a gay Hallingdal design, pictured above, on the back of a hand mirror and match box. The mirror frame, made of clear pine, is 10½ inches long, 5¼ inches across the round end, and ½ inch thick. You can buy a similar one or cut one with a jigsaw or saber saw, following the pattern in Figure B, page 1804. The floral design has few details and can be used on many objects, including not only the matchbox, but a box lid, a small plate, or a shallow nut bowl.

To decorate the mirror frame, first give it two coats of background color. (Red is a favorite in Hallingdal-style painting.) Transfer the pattern (Figure C, page 1804) to the mirror frame, following the chalk method described in the Craftnotes opposite. Have the paint medium prepared (page 1800) and the tools and brushes handy. Mix the oil paints by following the color key at right, beneath the top picture.

With the water color brush, paint the center of the flower form dark blue, using C-shaped curves to fill in the large area. Next, paint the five white flower petals. The first stroke in each petal is straight down the center; the others are C-shaped curves filling in the sides. To shade the petals near the center of the flower, pull out a little of the blue color into the white. Do this by starting each petal brush stroke about ⅛ inch into the blue (photograph 6).

If you make a mistake and paint white too far into the background area, you can remove the excess with a white vinyl eraser (photograph 7). Wipe the eraser clean after each swipe to avoid any streaking. You could also use a brush dipped in turpentine and wiped dry, but some of the turpentine might remain to smear the paint and cause runs. I find a vinyl eraser neater and easier to use.

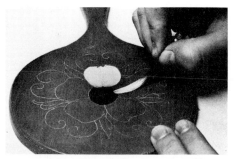

6: To shade the petals of the central flower form, load the brush with white paint and barely touch it into the wet center of dark blue; then pull it toward you. Do this at the beginning of each stroke in each petal.

7: You can use a white vinyl eraser to remove any white paint that strays outside the petal area. But most unevenness will be covered by the dark overlays that follow.

8: Hold the small scroller brush perpendicular to the mirror back when you paint the black overlays. Make a fist of your other hand to support the hand holding the brush.

9: To correct a mistake by lifting a dark color off a light background, pull a brush loaded with the light paint through the mistake, stroking in the direction opposite to the original stroke. Clean the brush; then repeat with the light color.

10: Be careful to keep your fingers still and let your wrist control the curve when you paint the curled tendrils. This is an exception—all other strokes are controlled by the fingers.

11: Highlight the leaf forms on the top edges with two white C-shaped curves. Define the opposite sides sharply with thin black lines.

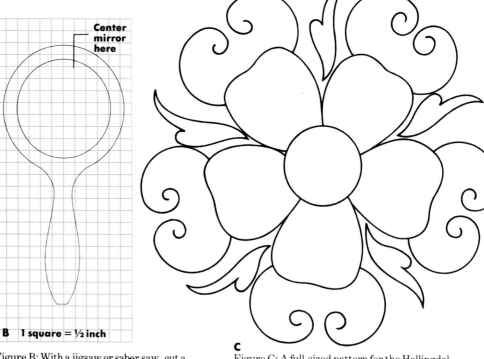

Center mirror here

B 1 square = ½ inch

C

Figure B: With a jigsaw or saber saw, cut a mirror frame from ½-inch-thick clear pine. Enlarge the pattern by making a grid of ½-inch squares and copying the shape of the frame on your grid, one square at a time. Cut out the pattern, outline it with pencil on the wood, and cut.

Figure C: A full-sized pattern for the Hallingdal design of the mirror back is given above. Only the basic, first-layer shapes are shown; overlays and individual details can be seen in the step-by-step and color photographs. For methods of transferring this pattern, see Craftnotes, page 1802.

Now switch to the scroller brush and thin ivory black to paint the overlays that outline the petal shapes. These overlays do not appear on the pattern. You paint them freehand, varying the width from thick in the middle to thin at the ends, as shown in the photographs. Rest the hand holding the brush on your other hand, and keep the brush perpendicular to the surface being painted (photograph 8). Paint slowly to give the paint time to flow smoothly down and off the brush. Then, with the same brush, paint clusters of three small teardrops inside each petal. Again, these accent strokes are not given on the pattern because they are done freehand; follow the photographs and your own artistic sense for placement. Start at the base of the petal and make the center teardrop almost straight. The two outer teardrops that swing to the sides should be shorter than the center one to give the illusion of curvature to the petal.

If a dark teardrop goes astray on the white petal, lift it off instead of trying to cover it up. To do this, load the watercolor brush with white paint, and turn the mirror around so that when you pull the brush toward you, you will be pulling toward the center of the flower. Push the brush down and into the mistake; then pull it toward yourself, thus lifting off the dark color (photograph 9). Clean the brush and go over the area again with white. You could use a cotton-tipped swab in the same manner, but you need to make sure it does not leave fuzz clinging to the wet paint.

This design is worked from the center out; so the next step is to paint the dark green leaves between the petals, using the watercolor brush. Each leaf is made with two S-shaped strokes, one long and one short, placed side by side.

Switch back to the scroller brush to paint the black tendrils that curl out from the flower. You can also add teardrops inside the tendrils, as Julie did (photograph 10).

White accent strokes are added to highlight dark areas, adding a sunlit feeling and giving the background a lively look. With the scroller, make clusters of white dots outside the tendrils and a ring of dots inside the center of the flower. Then highlight each leaf form with two C-shaped curves on the top side (photograph 11). Give each leaf further definition with a thin, black shadow line on the opposite side.

Let the paint dry thoroughly; then rub off any chalk lines that still show. Turn the frame over and glue a 4-inch-round mirror on the face.

The Norwegian words for "Give us this day our daily bread" frame the Hallingdal design on this wooden bread board. The painted side is strictly decorative; the back side is lightly oiled and can be used for cutting purposes.

Color key

Dark green	One part cadmium yellow light; two parts ivory black; and two parts raw umber
Light green	One part dark green; one part old white; and two parts cadmium yellow light
Light red	Equal parts of cadmium red light and burnt sienna
Dark red	Add more burnt sienna to light red
Old white	Titanium white with just a bit of raw sienna and raw umber
Putty beige	Add more raw sienna and raw umber to old white
Gold	Equal parts of raw sienna; cadmium yellow deep; and titanium white

A close-up view of the floral design of the bread board can be used as a guide for placement of colors and the overlay strokes that are not indicated on the basic pattern on page 1806.

Designs and Decorations
"Our daily bread" board ¢ ⊠ ⚐ 🐀

The design on the bread board pictured above is also done in the Hallingdal style—the flower forms are the same as those used on the mirror frame—but it is more elaborate, with graceful scrolls that are shaded from light to dark. This is an exception to the usual style, which is without such elaborate scrolls.

Start with an unfinished hard-maple bread board that measures about 8 inches wide and 11 inches long (minus the handle). Paint the front side and the edges with two coats of blue-green latex enamel. Leave the back unpainted; you will use only that side for cutting. Transfer the patterns for the Norwegian words (Figure D, page 1806) and the design (Figure E, page 1806) onto the painted side, using the chalk method described in the Craftnotes, page 1802. Follow the photographs above for placement of colors and details. Have the thinning medium prepared (page 1800) and the tools and brushes handy. Mix the oil paints by following the color key at right.

With the watercolor brush, paint the three flower forms at top center. Paint their centers a deep, rust red and make three thick, straight strokes for each white petal. Pull a bit of color out from the center into the petals, as described in the preceding project. Paint only the basic shapes; let details wait until later.

Next, move down to the central shape on the bottom half of the board. In rosemaling, you should paint from light to dark when two or more colors are placed side by side. Therefore, paint the white scalloped section before you add the gold.

1805

D
Figure D: A full-sized pattern for the Norwegian words meaning "Give us this day our daily bread" is given above. Center the first three words above and the second three words below the central design on the board.

Center of design; flop pattern over for right side.

Figure E: One half of a full-sized pattern for the Hallingdal design used on the bread board is given above. Flop your tracing to get a pattern for the right half. For methods of transferring this pattern, see Craftnotes, page 1802. Only basic shapes are given; follow the color photographs on page 1805 for the placement of overlays and details.

Move on to the scrolls that extend outward on both sides; be sure to keep turning the board so you are always painting toward yourself. Do the light green scrolls first, then the dark green (photograph 12). Even the longest scroll must be painted in one continuous stroke; support your hand with your little finger to make this

12: Keep turning the board so that you are always stroking toward yourself. In the case of plant forms such as these leaf scrolls, turn the board so that your strokes follow the direction of natural growth from base to tip.

13: Even the longest scroll must be painted in one continuous stroke if you are to achieve the smooth, gracefully flowing lines that are a basic characteristic of rosemaling. You can steady your hand with your little finger.

14: Broad highlights can be painted with the larger watercolor brush instead of the scroller; the hand position is the same. Here a bridge—a strip of thin plywood resting on two blocks—supports the hand and prevents smearing.

15: Black outlines and accents not shown on the pattern are painted after the basic shapes are completed. Use the color photographs as guides.

16: Script lettering is done with the scroller. The technique is much like writing with a nibbed pen; upstrokes are thin, downstrokes are broader.

easier (photograph 13). To blend the light and the dark bands into a medium green where they meet, clean the brush, apply enough pressure to flatten it as soon as it touches down, and pull it along the line where the two colors meet, thus stroking them together. (Rosemaling experts also do shading by loading two colors, side by side, on a large, flat brush, but this requires great dexterity and much practice.)

You can paint one half of the design at a time, as shown, or paint segments of both sides in sequence, working from the center out. After the green scrolls, paint the light and dark red scrolls below them, in the same manner as described for the green. Then fill in the light and dark green and light red areas in the center between the scrolls. First paint only the basic shapes given in the pattern; again, outlines and accents will be painted later as overlays. The smaller three-petal gold flowers and the flowers with small balls for petals are painted next.

With the basic design completed, you are ready to highlight the scrolls. Notice that the green scrolls are highlighted with white and the red scrolls are highlighted with gold. Use a flat wooden stick (a yardstick or paint stirrer works well) and two blocks of wood (higher than the bread board) to make a bridge that will support your hand while keeping it off the freshly painted areas nearby. These highlighting strokes are thick and important; continue to use the larger brush but keep it perpendicular with the board (photograph 14).

Fill in the leaves for the three flowers on top with green. Then give them stems and outside teardrops with the scroller brush, using thin ivory black paint. With the same brush and paint, add the accent lines shown in photograph 15 and the color photographs on page 1805.

The script lettering is usually done last, though in photograph 16, for demonstration purposes, it was done before the second half of the floral motif was completed. It is painted the way you write, with thin upstrokes and pressure on the thicker downstrokes, enough to widen out the brush. Again, support your hand with the bridge and use the vertical-brush technique used for accent lines.

Let the design paint dry thoroughly; then rub off any chalk lines that remain. Turn the board over and rub the unpainted side lightly with mineral oil.

Color key

Dark blue	One part Prussian blue; one-half part burnt umber; four parts ivory black; two parts titanium white
Light blue	Add dark blue to titanium white (see the note on page 1802)
Gold	Equal parts of raw sienna; cadmium yellow deep; yellow ocher; and old white
Dark red	Equal parts of cadmium yellow light; cadmium red light; and burnt sienna
Light red	Add titanium white to dark red
Dark green	Equal parts of cadmium yellow light; raw umber; and ivory black
Light green	Equal parts of dark green; cadmium yellow light; and old white

17: Paint the major scrolls first, one at a time. The sequence to follow is this: First paint the light color, then the dark color beside it, then blend the two together where they meet.

18: After painting the light blue areas of the petals, load the brush with dark blue paint without wiping off the light blue that remains. Start at the outside of the dark area and move toward the light for a gradual shading; then blend the two where they meet.

19: Each small white ball in the center of the flower motif is started at the outside edge. As you pass the dark green center, lightly touch it with the brush, swirling a bit of green into the white.

Norwegian rosemalers never painted their everyday dishes, only decorative ones that were often displayed behind plate rails on walls or in cupboards. A rimmed plate like this, with an intricately scrolled Telemark design, might merit a similar place of honor in your home.

Designs and Decorations
Telemark in the round

An asymmetrical Telemark design of intertwining scrolls stands out effectively on the chalk-white wooden plate pictured above. An inch-wide rim, painted blue and decorated with a thin, black, rope design, frames the central design.

The plate shown has a center area about 8 inches in diameter. Paint the plate with two coats of latex enamel—white on the center front, soft blue on the back and rim. Transfer the pattern (Figure F) using graphite transfer paper as described in the Craftnotes, page 1802. Have the thinning medium prepared (page 1800) and the tools and brushes handy. To mix the oil paints, follow the color key at top left.

When painting Telemark designs, the sequence is important. Paint the major shapes first, starting with those that appear to be in the background and working forward to give depth to the design. Here, start with the scrolls because they are the most important elements, establishing the size and shape of the overall pattern. Because the border is blue, there are no blue scrolls, but there are touches of blue in the flower motifs.

Rather than painting the plate with it resting flat on your work surface, you can hold it at an angle with one hand and paint with the other. Using the watercolor brush, paint the scrolls one at a time so the paint does not start to dry before you do the edge-blending (photograph 17). On each one, first paint the lighter area (gold), then the darker (red), touching the gold but not overlapping it. To blend, wipe excess paint off the brush, flatten it, and pull it through the two colors where they meet, creating a mixed tone between them. After the scrolls, move on to the central flower form. Do the green leaves first, because they are behind the flower. Then do the blue petals, and finally the red and gold petals. All of these shapes are

F

Figure F: A full-sized pattern for the round plate's Telemark design is given above. For ways to transfer this pattern to the plate, see Craftnotes, page 1802. For placement of freehand details, see color photograph opposite.

painted in three steps: first, the light color; second, the dark color by its side; third, the blending of the two colors through the middle. Next, the single flowers emerging between the scrolls are painted and shaded (photograph 18).

The center of the large floral motif is made up of small balls. The center ball is dark green; the outer ones are old white, shaded into the dark green. To shade them, start each of the white balls at the outside edge; then brush slightly into the dark color as you pass the center ball, swirling a bit of the dark color into the light (photograph 19).

20: Thin black outlines and accents are painted with the scroller brush, held vertically. For the placement of these top layer accents, follow the color photograph on page 1808.

21: A chalked guideline will help you make an even border design. Hold your hand as shown so your fingers will keep the guideline spaced a uniform distance from the edge.

22: Paint the rope border design with the scroller. Each overlapping S-shaped curve is about 1 inch long, crossing the chalk line in the middle and touching it at both ends.

The thin black outlines and accent lines painted with the scroller are added last (photograph 20). Follow the color photograph on page 1808 for placement; these detail strokes are done freehand, so they are not indicated on the basic pattern.

To keep the rope design around the edge evenly spaced, scribe a chalk line midway around the rim. Hold the chalk so it touches the rim at midpoint and brace the fingers of that hand against the rim of the plate (photograph 21). As you turn the plate and hold your chalk hand still, an even line will be made. With the scroller and thin ivory black paint, make a series of interlocking, S-shaped curves, each about 1 inch long, all around the rim (photograph 22). Each S-shaped stroke begins and ends on the chalk line, crossing it in the middle and touching the neighboring strokes at their midway points. The stroke steps are: point, pressure, point, lift.

When the design paint is dry, rub off any chalk or graphite lines that show. You will probably want to sign this and other rosemaling pieces you paint. The scroller brush makes a line that is overpowering; instead, use a fine-point felt-tipped pen or a quill pen dipped in india ink.

This red-and-green treasure box is a miniature version of a Norwegian dowry chest. The color bands are intended to suggest metal bands. This box was antiqued with a glaze after the Telemark design was painted. The inside was painted red and given a mottled antique glaze.

Designs and Decorations
A treasure of a box

$ ● ♦ 🗲

Jewelry, photographs, even doll clothes—whatever you or someone you love considers a treasure—can be kept in this small-scale replica of a dowry chest.

First, paint the chest inside and out with two coats of the background colors you have chosen. Mark the side bands (about ¾ inch wide) and the center bands on the front and back (about 1¼ inches wide) with chalk. Mask them by putting architect's drafting tape outside their edges before you paint in the second color (photograph 23). Such tape does not lift the first coat of paint when it is removed, but you should take it off before the band paint is completely dry.

The inside of the chest can be a surprise color, perhaps one matching the outside bands. Give it one coat of a commercial glaze in an antique color over the two coats of bright color. Mottle the glaze while it is still wet by dabbing it with crumpled plastic wrap or aluminum foil (photograph 24).

When the inside paint is dry, tape the box closed and transfer the patterns for the lid design (Figure G, page 1812) and the front medallions (Figure H, page 1812), using the chalk method described in the Craftnotes, page 1802. Have the thinning medium prepared (page 1800) and the tools and brushes handy. Mix the oil paints following the color key, top right on the opposite page.

Paint the two front medallions first (photograph 25). You may need to paint standing up in order to be comfortable. Put your initial inside one medallion and the year in the other (see the color photographs at left and opposite).

Next, paint the lid. This Telemark design is similar to that on the plate (page 1808) and the painting technique is the same. Paint the major elements—the scrolls and the central motif—starting with the one that will appear to be the most in the

This close-up view of the lid design used on the treasure box will guide your choice of colors and help you place the black overlays and accents.

Color key	
Old white	Titanium white with just a bit of raw sienna and raw umber
Yellow	Equal parts of cadmium yellow light; cadmium yellow deep; raw sienna; and old white
Light green	Equal parts of cadmium yellow light and raw umber
Dark green	Equal parts of cadmium yellow light; raw umber, and ivory black
Red	Equal parts of burnt sienna; cadmium red light; and cadmium yellow light
Dark red	Two parts burnt sienna; one part cadmium red light; and one part cadmium yellow light
Light red	One part red and three parts old white

Follow this close-up when painting the front medallions; it shows the colors used and the placement of the overlay and accents. Paint your initials in one medallion and the year in the other; draw them with chalk before you paint them.

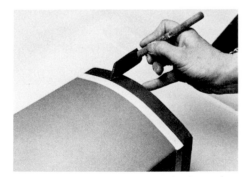

23: Paint the contrasting bands on the chest when the background color is dry, using a polyfoam brush. To get a straight edge, use architect's drafting tape for masking.

24: Paint a commercial glaze over the bright color to give the inside of the box an antique look. You can mottle the wet glaze by dabbing it with crumpled aluminum foil, plastic wrap, or your fingers.

25: Paint the front medallions on the treasure box before you paint the lid. You may have to paint standing up, supporting one hand with the other, in order to be at a comfortable height.

Left side

Top

G

**Center of design;
flop pattern over
for right side.**

Top

H

Figure G (above): This is one half of a full-sized pattern for the Telemark design on the lid of the treasure box. Flop your tracing to get a pattern for the right half. You can transfer the pattern to the box by following the chalk method given in the Craftnotes, page 1802. A full-sized pattern for the front medallions is given in Figure H. If either of these patterns is too large or too small for your box, you can have them reduced or enlarged at a photostat shop.

Figure H (left): This is a full-sized pattern for a medallion for the front of the treasure box. Transfer two to the box, one on either side of the center band. Medallions of this type are typical of the Telemark style of rosemaling.

26: On the box lid, paint the overlapping scrolls and the central motif first, laying on the light and dark colors side by side, then blending them together with a center stroke.

27: Curved cross-hatching lines create the illusion of contour in an area of the central motif that has not been painted with any design color. These black lines are painted with the scroller.

28: A thin black border of S-shaped curves, connected by diagonal dashes, outlines the bands. Use the scroller and support your hand on a bridge so you do not smear wet paint elsewhere.

background. Paint the light and dark colors side by side and blend (photograph 26). Paint the additional flower forms, then do the accenting. On this design, there is a space in the central motif that is not painted, so the background color shows through. This area is accented with curved cross-hatching lines that give the illusion of a contour. Use a bridge to support your hand as you paint the curved lid (photograph 27).

A border design of S-shaped curves and diagonal dashes outlines the bands (photograph 28). Practice this design first on a piece of painted cardboard to be sure you have mastered it before you paint it on the box.

When the paint is dry, rub off any chalk lines that still show, and add decorative hardware such as the handles and lock plate. If you like, you can antique the box to mellow and age the colors (see Craftnotes, below).

For related entries, see "Antiquing," "Oil Painting," and "Tin Painting."

CRAFTNOTES: ANTIQUING

Any object that has been painted with a rosemaling design can be antiqued, but this technique of simulating aging is more appropriate for some designs than others. The treasure box—because of its size, shape, colors, and the fact that it resembles an antique dowry chest—is a good choice for antiquing. After the design paint has dried for about a week and a half, rub the entire chest lightly with 0000 steel wool (above). Rub more on the corners and edges that would naturally show more wear, and do not hesitate to take off a little paint. Your goals are to make the chest look old and to smooth the surface, making it more receptive to the antiquing glaze. The antiquing glaze can be a commercial brand, a solution of green-umber pow-

dered pigment with medium, or even the scrapings from your palette that you have saved and mixed together. Stir the glaze well and wipe it onto the chest with a soft rag (above); wear a rubber glove.

Immediately wipe off excess glaze with a soft, clean rag, leaving the glaze darker in some areas, especially near the bands. Wipe the bands separately in a front-to-back motion, leaving them streakier than the rest of the box (center, bottom). (Ideally, you would antique the box before you added the hardware. If the handles are already on, check occasionally for drips that may run out from underneath them.)

With your bare hand, rub the finish when it is completely dry to smooth any rough spots and to give the surface a mellow glow (above). Finish with two coats of semigloss varnish after the antiquing glaze is completely dry. Burnish the dry varnish with 0000 steel wool.

RUBBINGS
Shadows of the Past

You can reproduce the image of any incised or raised solid surface by covering it with thin paper and rubbing it with wax or ink. Archaeologists use rubbing techniques to record intricate details of ancient carvings, such as the Peruvian monolith on page 1817; historians and genealogists use rubbings to trace lineage by means of gravestones; artists, craftsmen, and collectors use rubbings to make decorative wall hangings. But these rubbings are only a modern version of an ancient Chinese art form called T'a-pen. The oldest rubbings that still exist date from 7 A.D. At that time rubbings served not only a decorative purpose but they were a simple way to print books from stones inscribed with text. During the twelfth century, the art of rubbing spread through Europe and the British Isles, where it became modish to make rubbings of monumental brass plaques in churches, such as the ones on page 1819. The rubbing shown in the photograph on page 1822 was taken from a wall of an ancient temple at Angkor Wat in Cambodia.

You do not have to be near an ancient shrine to make beautiful rubbings. Gravestones are a common source of images for rubbings. The motifs, religious symbols, and inscriptions on old gravestones, such as the one at lower right and on pages 1816 and 1821, yield exciting rubbings. For a contemporary look, you can rub manhole covers and other iron fittings with unwrapped wax crayons to produce a collage such as the one shown opposite. Using only a soft pencil and tracing paper, you may want to try your hand at making rubbings of some of the following: coins, ornate silverware, decorated door knobs, fossils, leaves, lace, ribbed cardboard, horse harness decorations, license plates, tire treads, cut glass, doilies, keys, or jewelry. Young and old alike can enjoy this craft, which requires only a few simple and inexpensive tools and materials.

Marie Heinbach started making rubbings while traveling through England. She teaches history at a junior high school in Brooklyn and a course in brass and stone rubbings for Brooklyn College's adult education program. When she is not in the classroom, Marie collects oak furniture, cooks, and reads mysteries.

Graphic Arts
Tombstone tracings

To obtain a sharp image from an incised, flat surface such as a gravestone, right, or a brass plaque (page 1818), use either a block of wax such as a heel ball (a mixture of wax and lampblack) or cake block wax—both available at art supply shops. Purists prefer to use white paper rubbed with a black heel ball, but many color combinations are possible. For example, black paper rubbed with a gold heel ball yields a striking pattern. In addition to the rubbing wax you will need: scissors; rags; a soft natural-bristle brush; an old cushion or towel; 24-by-36-inch sheets or a 40-inch-wide roll of student-grade rice paper or aquaba paper (also known as detail paper); masking tape; a long cardboard tube; and a moist cloth for clean-up.

But before you start making rubbings at the nearest cemetery, get permission from the proper authorities. Some places charge a fee; some even prohibit rubbings if the stones have been damaged by weathering, have historical significance, or have been marred by careless rubbers. In general, I have found that most officials are quite helpful. Just don't spoil the fun for others—leave the stone in the same condition that it was when you arrived.

Once you get approval, the time to rub is on a dry, sunny day when the wax will soften and rub easily onto the paper. First, walk about the graveyard looking at the symbols, names, and epitaphs inscribed on each stone until you find one that interests you. Later you may want to learn more about the motifs and the customs of the area to understand the meanings of early grave artists.

When you find an interesting and clearly cut stone, use scissors to remove any weeds that may be in the way. Brush away any bird droppings, lichen, or moss that

This dry-wax rubbing reproduces an urn-and-willow motif from an old tombstone. This design was popular with New England stone carvers of the early 1800s.

Something new to serve as a rubbing pattern is always under foot once you discover manhole covers and the water and fuel caps set into urban sidewalks. Various iron fittings, rubbed with unwrapped colored crayons, created the montage opposite.

1: Before doing a dry-wax rubbing of an incised stone or brass, use a soft nylon brush to wipe away any dirt that is on the surface. Spots that can't be removed will not detract from the design.

2: Cut rice paper slightly larger than the surface to be rubbed; then tape the paper over the center of the top edge. Pull the paper taut over the surface as you tape the bottom and side edges.

3: Use short, light, even strokes to block in a faint image of the design with rubbing wax. Study this to determine which areas of the design should receive the most attention.

4: A second rubbing with wax darkens the details of this tombstone in New York's Trinity church cemetery. The winged death's head with a frown reflects the fear of death instilled by the Puritanical religion of the early 1700s.

has discolored or obscured the stone engraving (photograph 1). But do not use any solvent in your effort to clean the stone; you may only make any discoloration worse or eat away part of the stone. Small blemishes and even the cracks on old stones made of sandstone or limestone will not spoil your rubbing.

Once the stone is brushed clean, put a cushion in front of it to protect your clothing and keep you as comfortable as possible. If you are going to make a lot of rubbings, you will find the pad will help keep your knees from getting stiff and sore.

Cut a piece of rice paper 2 inches larger all around than the stone, so that no wax will mar the surface of the stone. First tape the paper to the center of the stone's top edge with masking tape. Then pull the paper taut and tape it to the bottom of the stone (photograph 2). Mold the paper to the contour of the top by pulling and taping it in place. If necessary, attach extra pieces of tape along the sides to make sure that the paper is stretched tautly across the surface. (Never use clear tape; it can damage stones and brasses.) If the paper shifts while you are rubbing, a shadow image or blurred image will result. Rub wax onto the taped paper with your hand; the wax will rub off wherever the paper comes into direct contact with the surface of the design beneath. But any incised or cut-away areas on the stone will remain white on the completed rubbing.

Prior to rubbing, carry the wax in a pocket or in the palm of your hand so it will soften a bit from body heat. This makes it stick better to the paper. Use the broad, flat edge of the rubbing wax to block in the basic design on the paper with light, even strokes (photograph 3). Study this faint image to check any areas that are not transferring properly and to select parts of the design that you want to darken or leave lighter than others. With this foundation, darken the design by rubbing the wax over the paper with a small, circular motion (photograph 4). Avoid using hard-edged strokes or pressing too hard at this stage; either can spoil the soft, aged look you are seeking in the finished rubbing. As you work, the ball of wax should develop sharp corners and straight edges. You can use them to reach into any crannies around the engraved design. Straight edges are handy when you need a piece of wax broad enough to fit across the width of a letter without leaving wax marks on its inner edges. When you work over letters, be sure to rub up and down along the length of the letters to avoid catching chunks of wax on the letter edges.

When you have outlined and darkened the letters and motifs to your satisfaction, take a break. Study the rubbing from a distance before you take it off the stone. Since the rubbing will look lighter indoors than it does in the sunlight, you may want to compensate for this by going over some areas of the design again. When you are satisfied, remove the tape from the bottom and the side edges first, then from the top of the stone by pulling the tape out toward the stone's edge. Record the place and date of the rubbing (with a pencil) in the lower right-hand corner. Then roll the paper loosely and put it in a cardboard tube for protection.

If you happen to get an unwanted wax build-up at any spot on the rubbing, you can fix it later with a single-edged razor blade, scraping carefully so you just graze the surface of the wax. Then retouch the spot, using the same circular motion so the wax matches the rest of the rubbed surface. Areas can be darkened by neutralizing the wax with extract of ox gall (available at art supply stores), then applying india ink. Any smudge spots along the edge of the rice paper can be hidden with white ink.

The monolith of the Great Spear, believed to represent universal man, was hidden for perhaps 3,000 years in a temple cave in the province of Ancash, Peru. Archaeologists of the *Asociacion de Artes y Estudios Experimentales* used carbon-paper rubbings to transfer the symbolic birds, cats, and serpents, intricately engraved in the stone onto tracing paper. Carbon rubbings, although somewhat light, are sharper and more detailed than a photograph of the surface would be.

This is a composite of carbon rubbings taken from the monolith pictured at top, right. By arranging the rubbings in sequence as they were taken from both sides of the stone, the archaeologists were able to interpret the engravings. To make a carbon rubbing, tracing paper is taped to the stone, then covered with carbon paper, inked side down, and a sheet of newsprint. A piece of shoe leather or the bowl of a wooden spoon is used to rub all three layers at once to transfer the image.

Alice Richard is a dentist and writer who lives in Michigan. Alice grew up in England, where she began her study of monumental brasses. Her husband and teen-aged son and daughter share her fascination with medieval monuments such as those pictured below and opposite.

Graphic Arts
Brass rubbings

In Europe, especially Britain, you can find splendid monumental brasses in country churches as well as cathedrals, all suitable for rubbing. Brasses varying in size from a few inches to more than 6 feet long are set in walls and floors, sometimes beneath pews (be careful not to step on the brasses). Incised brass plates designed as tomb markers offer a glimpse into medieval times: knights in armor, merchants and their families, ecclesiastical figures, and noblemen, all richly decorated with heraldic animals, shields, crests, canopies, or inscriptions such as those in the photographs opposite. Dry-wax rubbings on detail paper reproduce them so faithfully that they are sought after as pin-ups (photograph 5 and the completed rubbings shown opposite). Inexpensive paperbacks and free literature provided by British art suppliers list the locations of the more popular of Britain's monumental brasses.

Permission to rub should always be obtained from a church official, preferably in writing and well ahead of the busy tourist season, May through August. A modest fee is usually charged at the time of rubbing. Be thoughtful; the poor manners of a few tourists have led some churchmen to view the popularity of brass rubbing as a mixed blessing.

Allow two hours to rub a large brass, using the same technique described for making a tombstone rubbing. When you have finished every detail, remove the rubbing and brush away any loose wax. If you like, you can use a nylon stocking to go over the rubbing to give the wax a gloss.

5: You can use the dry-wax method to rub incised brasses such as this one of Dame Ratcliffe Wingfield, All Saints' Church, Easton, Suffolk, England (1601). Using masking tape, secure a sheet of detail paper over the brass; then rub heel-ball wax over the design from top to bottom, using small, straight strokes. Work your way slowly down the brass, reproducing every detail.

A finished rubbing can be mounted on a cardboard sheet of the same size, using white glue or masking tape. Then make a mat from another piece of white or colored cardboard, using a craft knife and ruler to cut an opening the size of the rubbing plus as much of the border as you want to show. For maximum protection, frame the matted rubbing under nonglare glass.

To make a decorative wall hanging, cut a piece of fabric such as linen, burlap, or calico 6 inches larger than the rubbing on all edges. Press the side edges under 2 inches and sew with a basting stitch. Then fold the top and bottom edges under 2 inches and sew a hem, using a running stitch and leaving the ends open. Cut a piece of felt and a piece of clear, thin plastic acetate the same size as the rubbing. Using scissors, cut an opening in the felt to make a mat that will conceal all or part of the border around the rubbing. Put four strips of double-faced tape on the back of the felt mat along its edges. Tape the felt to the acetate. Then center the rubbing on the backing fabric, and put the felt mat and acetate over it. Use a running stitch to sew through all four layers to hold them together. Insert a wooden lath or a 1¾-inch-thick dowel into the top and bottom hems. For hanging, tie a decorative cord around each end of the top dowel, using a tassel to hide the knotted ends of the cord.

This image of Sir Roger Trumpington (1289) was rubbed from a monumental brass in Trumpington, near Cambridge, England.

Craftswoman Alice Richard transferred this rubbing of Richard, Isabel, and John Manfeld (1455) from a brass plate at St. Nicholas' Church in Taplow, Berkshire, England. All three children died before their parents did. John Manfeld (right) is dressed in swaddling clothes, indicating that he died as an infant. Isabel died at a young age; her long hair is a symbol of virginity.

This rubbing was taken from the brass of Sir Edmund Flambard (1370) at St. Mary's Church in Harrow, Middlesex, England the remaining portion of a larger brass that also pictured his wife. A brass of their son can still be seen next to Sir Edmund's in the chancel.

St. Michael's Church in St. Albans, Hertfordshire, England, displays the popular brass from which this rubbing was taken, picturing John and Maud Pecok (1380). This early brass is unusual because it depicts civilians; other brasses of this time commonly commemorate knights in armor.

Gail Summers was graduated from Brooklyn College with a master's degree in art education. She teaches art at Dewey Junior High School in Brooklyn. After hours, Gail and Marie Heinbach organize expeditions to rubbing sites or exhibit their finished rubbings at craft fairs, under the name of City Textures.

Graphic Arts
Inking raised designs

Although the dry-wax method works well on an incised design, it is hard to use on a raised design without catching wax in the grooves. Wet ink is a better medium for rubbing reliefs such as those on the stone below and the brass on page 1823.

To make the stone rubbing, I used permanent black boku-taku ink, available at art supply stores, but I suggest that you use water-soluble inks. They come in a variety of colors and can easily be removed with water if any ink soaks through the paper onto the stone. In addition you will need these materials: 24-by-36-inch sheets or a 40-inch-wide roll of student-grade rice paper or aquaba paper; a spray bottle or plant mister; a canteen; a soft bristle brush; scissors; masking tape; a cushion; an old terry cloth towel; a cardboard tube; rags; two 2-inch-wide sponge balls or wads of cotton; six 6-by-6-inch squares of muslin or cotton fabric; four 6-by-6-inch squares of silk, organdy, or nylon; and two rubber bands or twist ties.

To get a head start at home, prepare two dabbers for applying the ink. To make a dabber, stack three squares of cotton cloth or muslin evenly over two pieces of nylon. Then place a ball of cotton or a sponge in the center of the cloth pile. Pull the cloth taut over the soft center, and tie it very tightly so the cloth will not come loose as you use the dabber. Smaller dabbers are useful for reaching narrow spaces. Next, fill a canteen and an empty spray bottle with water.

Select a stone or brass of low to medium relief, such as the one shown below (photograph 6). (Stones of high relief require the technique described on page 1823.) Clean the surface of the design. Then cut the paper and tape it over the stone as shown on page 1816. Use the spray bottle to mist the paper over the center of the motif, applying water with a circular motion (photograph 7). Then use a damp terry cloth towel or clean fingers to pat the moist paper gently, molding it to the contours of the raised design (photograph 8). Be sure to press out all air bubbles and eliminate any wrinkles from the paper. Spray additional areas of the paper, working from the center of the stone to its outer edges, until the entire area to be inked is damp and pressed to the stone. Dampening and pressing the paper carefully are the keys to successful inking. How wet you make the paper depends on the consistency of your ink and on the print shading that you like. Generally, thicker ink calls for wetter paper; if you use a thin ink, let the paper get nearly dry.

6: This smiling winged cherub was carved in the mid-1700s, indicating a shift from the fear of death to the joy of anticipated resurrection.

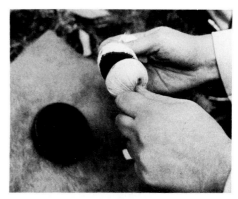

7: Here an incised epitaph has already been transferred with dry wax; then the raised area at the top was misted for inking.

8: The key to successful inking lies in pressing the damp paper carefully with your fingers to establish the outlines of the raised areas.

9: Dip a dabber in ink. Then rub it with another dabber, transferring the excess ink. Use only the second dabber to ink the raised areas.

Next, prepare to apply ink. Dip one dabber in the ink; then rub it against another to transfer excess ink (photograph 9). The second dabber is the one with which you will ink the paper. If your dabber has too much ink on it, you can get blots on your paper. It is better to start with too little ink and add more as you get used to the method. You can test how much ink you have on the dabber on a piece of scrap paper before you start the rubbing.

Gently pat the inked dabber on the rice paper you have molded over the raised features of the design (photograph 10). Gently feel the outline of the stone or brass, and use short, circular motions to block in the design lightly. You will be able to see the design clearly when it is lightly inked. Do not let the dabber rest on the paper as this can create blots. When you run out of ink, repeat the inking procedure, removing excess ink by rubbing two dabbers together. Go over the design a second time to darken it, being careful to ink only the raised area as shown in photograph 11. Continue to moisten the paper if it starts to dry. When you have finished, let the paper and ink dry thoroughly before removing the rubbing from the stone, so you don't smudge the design. Remove the tape from along the bottom and top, pulling toward the outer edge; then slowly peel the rubbing off the stone. Write the place and date on the rubbing; then roll it up and store it in the cardboard tube. It can be prepared for display as described on page 1819.

10: Lightly pat the raised areas with the dabber. Spray more water onto the paper if it starts to get dry. Apply ink to the raised areas of the design until the rubbing is as dark as you wish.

11: Areas of low relief on stone or brass require that ink be applied to moistened paper. Incised designs covering the lower portions of this stone were rubbed with dry wax.

You can attach an inked rubbing to a folded sheet of colored paper, making an attractive greeting card. Cut around the edges of a rubbing and center it on the folded paper; then use white glue to fasten it in place. Use scissors to make decorative cut-outs along the fold.

The source of this rubbing, entitled *The Giant Ravana on His Chariot*, dates back to the eleventh century. French archaeologists took this rubbing from the pink sandstone bas-reliefs lining a temple wall of Angkor Wat in Cambodia. To reproduce the large panel, several damp sheets of rice paper were pounded together; the paper was positioned on the wall and backed with a piece of felt. Then a wooden mallet was used to hammer the paper until areas of relief were established. When the paper was almost dry, it was dabbed with Chinese ink.

High reliefs such as the bronze doors of the Cathedral of Saint John the Divine in New York City can be reproduced with ink rubbing—with the permission of the proper authorities. These doors depict scenes from the Old and New Testaments.

12: When you are rubbing areas of high relief, you will need to tape the paper securely on all edges before you moisten it.

13: Put powdered pigment in a plastic container, and slowly add linseed oil, stirring to combine them until the mixture has a creamy consistency.

Graphic Arts
Reproducing high reliefs

Stones or brasses of high relief can be inked successfully with a special technique. To transfer images from the brass doors of the cathedral in the photograph above, I applied ink to rice paper with a cloth. A rubbing made this way requires these materials: rags; masking tape; 24-by-36-inch sheets or a 40-inch-wide roll of student-grade rice paper or aquaba paper; jar of graphite powder or colored powdered pigment; can of linseed oil; spoon or ice cream stick; small plastic container; scissors; linen cloth; empty spray bottle; canteen filled with water; pencil; and cardboard tube.

To begin, use a clean rag to remove any dirt on the raised surface. Then cut a piece of rice paper slightly larger than the area to be rubbed. Tape the paper on all edges as you pull it taut over the relief (photograph 12). With the spray bottle, mist the paper with a circular motion until it is damp all over. Use your fingers to press the moist paper into the outlines of the raised areas as shown on page 1821. Then mix a small quantity of graphite powder or colored pigment with a small quantity of linseed oil, stirring with a spoon until the ink has a creamy consistency (photograph 13). Wrap a small linen cloth around your forefinger and dip it into the ink. Be careful not to pick up too much ink. Wipe off any excess ink on the lip of the container (photograph 14). Using short strokes, lightly rub ink over the raised surface to block in the overall design (photograph 15). Then continue to darken the design, dabbing ink over the raised areas with short, circular motions. Once the rubbing is as dark as you wish, let the ink dry thoroughly. Then remove the rubbing by pulling the tape toward the outer edge. Record the date and place of the rubbing with a pencil along the bottom edge of the paper. Then roll the rubbing and store it in a cardboard tube.

For related entries, see "Framing," "Greeting Cards," and "Monoprinting."

14: Wrap a linen cloth around your forefinger. Dip the cloth in the ink mixture, wiping off any excess on the lip of the container before you apply ink to the raised areas.

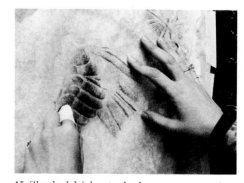

15: Slowly dab ink onto the damp paper, covering the raised areas until you have blocked out the entire design. Repeat the inking until the design is as dark as you wish.

RYA AND FLOSSA
Piles of Yarn

Once used solely to provide protection against the cold, rya is an ancient yarn knotting technique that is used today to create a deep, shaggy wool pile of subtle, lustrous colors. The length of the pile can vary from ½ inch to as much as 6 inches. Although the term flossa is used in Sweden to designate a short pile, the rya and flossa knotting techniques are identical. Rya, pronounced *ree-ah*, is a modern Swedish word generally applied to shaggy-pile rugs.

The use of pile for warmth probably began with efforts to simulate animal fur by sewing clumps of wool to clothing or bedcovers. Pile-lined textiles have survived from civilizations as old and as varied as those of the ancient Egyptians and the Vikings. The first ryas were monochromatic or had simple striped designs. They were put to many uses such as lap robes, clothing, bedcovers, and rugs, and were hung in open doorways to block drafts. Many examples of Scandinavian ryas made long ago can be seen at the *Norsk Folkemuseum* in Oslo, Norway and at the *Nordiska Museet* in Stockholm, Sweden.

As more efficient means of keeping warm were developed, the rya began to be used less for warmth than for visual and tactile pleasure. Changing aesthetic values allowed designers to make the most of the rich textures and colors of the yarns available. Although the knotting technique is most commonly used in rugs, the plushy rya surface that changes color and texture so intriguingly is often put to other uses, as in wall hangings (page 1826), pillows (opposite), and toys (page 1834).

The Loom or the Woven Backing

The rya pile may be formed in two ways. The traditional way is to work on a loom, using fingers to knot lengths of yarn onto the warp (lengthwise threads). Thus, the rya is knotted and the backing fabric is woven at the same time. In Scandinavia, people have been making ryas on looms for hundreds of years and continue to do so today. But a more modern method calls for using a large needle to knot the yarn onto a prewoven fabric backing.

Both techniques have advantages and disadvantages. A large loom represents a large initial expenditure, but the materials it uses are less expensive than a prewoven backing. In addition, using a loom allows great flexibility. You can vary the number of knots in a row and the distance between rows to achieve many different textures. You can also combine shaggy pile with areas of flat weaving, an option that opens many design possibilities. A disadvantage is the need to acquire two skills—weaving and knotting. And loom work, obviously, is not portable.

It is easy to work on a prewoven backing (photograph 1), and the work progresses quickly since the backing has already been woven. This technique requires very little in the way of equipment; you need only a large needle and basic sewing supplies. The work is portable, since the backing is held in the lap. The method's drawbacks —the cost of the special rya backing and the fact that the number of knots per row and the distance between rows is established—can, in many instances, be minimized. For example, on certain projects a less expensive backing called jute *aida* can be used. The wall hanging, page 1826, and the pillows, opposite, illustrate how imaginatively short dense pile, long shaggy pile, and needlepoint can be combined to counteract the monotony that a predetermined number of knots per row and rows per inch imposes. Another thing to consider before you decide which method to use is the appeal, for you, of the two techniques. If you like to weave, you are likely to prefer a loom. If you enjoy needlework, you probably will prefer forming the knots with a needle on a backing—a process related to embroidery.

Maggie Quitko (left) and Carla Faust Guiffreda are two of the three owners of Coulter Studios, a New York shop that sells imported yarns and equipment related to yarn crafts. Ms. Quitko, formerly a textile designer, became intrigued with rya knotting while traveling in Scandinavia. She created the projects here that were worked on special rya backing —the wall hanging, the pillows, and the rug. Ms. Guiffreda studied English literature in California. Her interest in yarn crafts began when she learned to crochet; she then learned knitting, macramé, embroidery, and weaving. She designed and made the woven rya cat pictured on page 1834.

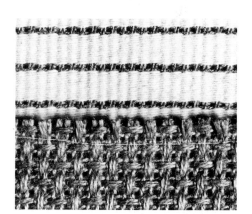

1: The two best backings to use for making rya knots with a tapestry needle are (top) imported rya backing and (bottom) jute *aida*.

Rya, a knotting technique, is most often utilized to make shaggy pile rugs. But soft, lustrous pillows can also be made. The top pillow combines rya pile with bargello stitches, a form of needlepoint. The bottom pillow gets its rippled texture from rows of long, knotted rya pile alternating with shorter flossa pile. Directions for the pillows begin on page 1828.

This rya wall hanging measures 32 by 59 inches and was worked with a large needle on a special prewoven rya backing fabric. The design is quite simple but the effect is striking due to the beauty of the yarns.

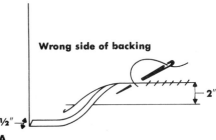

Wrong side of backing

½" 2"

A
Figure A: To hem the top and bottom edges of the rya backing fabric for a wall hanging, turn ½ inch and then 2 inches of the fabric to the wrong side. Sew the turned-under edge with tiny stitches.

Materials

Yarns: Scandinavian manufacturers produce special yarns for rya and flossa knotting. The yarns are made from long, sturdy fibers of pure wool. They are two-ply and have a distinctive ropelike twist. Rya yarns are available in glowing colors and come in two weights. Generally, the heavier weight is used for rugs and the lighter weight for pillows. For variety and special effects, other wool yarns may be mixed with rya yarns. These include Scotch or Finnish weaving wool, knitting worsted, fingering yarn, Persian yarn, and mohair. If it is available, try a type of yarn made of a blend of cowhair and wool. This yarn is imported from Norway, and although it is a one-ply yarn, it is just about as thick as rya rug yarn. For wall hangings and other works that will not be subject to much wear, experiment with other yarns and cords, such as cotton, linen, hand-spun yarn, unspun fleece, horsehair yarn, or silk. Experiment also with synthetic yarns and threads. Some designers even use raffia or strips of plastic to form the rya pile. If you decide to use different types of yarn simultaneously in the needle, make sure you cut each strand the same length.

Backings: Imported Scandinavian rya backing and jute *aida*, the two best backing fabrics to use, are shown in photograph 1, page 1825. The rya backing is sold by the yard and comes in widths ranging from 14 to 47 inches. It is heavy, woven fabric with narrow openwork rows spaced at ½-inch intervals. In these openwork rows, the vertical threads of the weave are exposed; it is over these exposed threads that the rya knots are made. Because this rya backing is very strong, it should be used for all rugs and large hangings. Jute *aida*, which is less expensive, can often be substituted for rya backing. This is rough, burlaplike fabric, with an open, even weave. It is sold by the yard and is usually 48 inches wide. Because it is more loosely woven than rya backing, it is a flimsier backing, and should be used only for small hangings (a large hanging would eventually sag and stretch out of shape) and items that will not receive much wear, such as decorative pillows.

Looms: A rya can be woven on any sturdy loom, from a simple frame that you can make yourself (page 1835) to a large floor loom. If you use a loom, you will also need a strong, tightly twisted yarn, capable of supporting the heavy weight of the pile, and a shuttle to carry the filler yarn.

Where to Buy Rya Supplies

Many needlecraft and weaving shops carry imported rya backings and yarn, and most will order materials that are not in stock. If you have difficulty finding materials, you can order supplies from Coulter Studios, Inc., 118 East 59th Street, New York, N.Y. 10022.

Needlecrafts
Wool cascades wall hanging $●👤🧶

The large wall hanging pictured (top, left) combines deep uncut loops of rya pile with short cut loops of flossa pile. The long tassels, added last, are wrapped with shiny rayon cord that contrasts with the texture of the wool yarns.

Materials

The 32-by-59-inch wall hanging requires rya rug yarn (3.6-ounce, 130-yard skeins) in the following amounts: five skeins each of three shades of rust-red (15 skeins total); one skein of ivory; and ten skeins of plum. (Choose other colors if you like.) You will also need a piece of 32-inch-wide rya backing 64 inches long; 11 yards of shiny rayon macramé cord in plum, ⅛ inch thick; heavy-duty sewing thread in white or beige; a No. 13 tapestry needle; a sewing needle; scissors; pencil; heavy paper; ruler (for enlarging the pattern); and a waterproof marker. To attach the finished hanging to the wall, use a 30-inch-long strip of so-called tackless stripping (available at carpet stores), finishing nails, and a hammer.

Making the Hanging

To make the hanging, first prepare the backing. With sewing thread, make a hem in the top and bottom edges by turning under ½ inch and then 2 inches (Figure A). Enlarge the pattern for the two semicircles (Figure B) and cut them out. Place the

In this detail of the rya wall hanging, you can see the contrast between the short, dense, cut flossa pile of the ivory-and-plum-colored areas (worked in every row) and the long, loose, shaggy, uncut loops of the rust-red rya pile (worked in every other row).

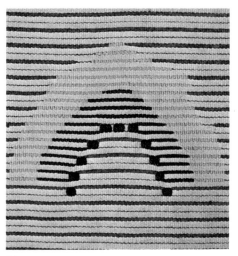

This back view of the rya wall hanging shows how rya knots look on the wrong side of the backing fabric. Each tassel is attached by pulling three sets of strands through three spaces that were left unworked, as well as through three spaces in the unworked row directly underneath.

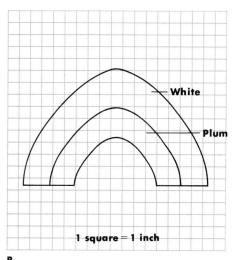

B

Figure B: To enlarge this pattern for the semicircles used in the wall hanging, copy it square by square on paper that you have ruled into 1-inch squares.

larger semicircle pattern on the right side of the backing, 4½ inches below the hemmed top edge and 8 inches in from each side (Figure C). Trace around this pattern with the waterproof marker. Remove the larger pattern and put the smaller semicircle pattern inside the outline of the larger one; then trace around its inside edge with the marker.

Next, prepare the yarn. Untwist each skein. Wind nine skeins of plum yarn into balls; they will be used to make the tassels. Cut the remaining skeins of yarn into strands approximately 56 inches long. To do this, cut through each skein once where the yarn is tied.

At this point, you can begin adding yarn to the backing. (Refer to the Craftnotes on page 1831 for instructions on how to make rya knots.) Because the hanging is large and will become heavier and more cumbersome as the work progresses, begin by working the plum semicircle first, then the ivory semicircle, then do the rust-red areas, rather than beginning at the bottom with rust-red.

To work the plum or ivory area, thread the needle with four strands of the color being used. Begin at the bottom left corner of each shape. Staying within the marked outline, make knots in every openwork row of the backing, forming 1-inch-long loops. Cut the loops after each row has been completed.

To work the rust-red areas, thread the needle with three strands of yarn—one strand of each shade. Begin knotting at the second openwork row from the bottom, penetrating only the top layer of the backing (not the hem) and forming uneven loops 2 to 3 inches long. Leave these loops uncut. Do not work the area that will be concealed by the tassels (Figure C). To allow for attaching the tassels later, skip the first row and skip three openwork spaces at the beginning and end of each row of rust-red worked within the plum-colored semicircle as shown in the photograph of the back of the hanging (above, right).

There are 11 tassels; cut, attach, and wrap the yarn for one tassel at a time, beginning with the three top tassels and working downward at each side. Each tassel consists of three sets of nine 118-inch-long strands of plum wool. To begin a tassel, measure and cut one set of strands. Thread the tapestry needle with the nine strands, and working from the front of the tapestry, insert the needle in one of the three openwork spaces allotted for that tassel (Figure D, page 1828). Pass the needle under the woven band of the backing, and bring it out through the openwork space directly below. Pull the yarn through, making the ends even in length. You now have nine doubled strands, for a total of 18. Attach two more sets of nine strands in the same way, making a total of 54 strands in each tassel. To wrap the tassel, thread the tapestry needle with a yard of rayon cord. Wrap the cord around

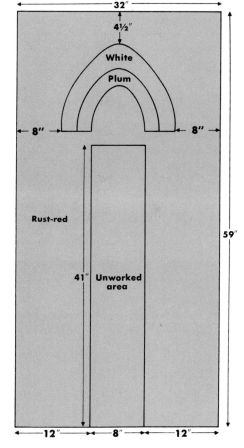

C

Figure C: Follow this diagram, measuring with a ruler, to position the semicircular patterns on the rya backing. To save yarn and time, mark the 8-by-41-inch area that will be hidden under the tassels and leave it unworked.

1827

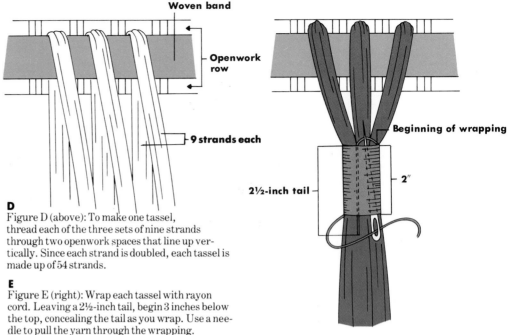

Woven band

Openwork row

9 strands each

Beginning of wrapping

2½-inch tail

2″

D
Figure D (above): To make one tassel, thread each of the three sets of nine strands through two openwork spaces that line up vertically. Since each strand is doubled, each tassel is made up of 54 strands.

E
Figure E (right): Wrap each tassel with rayon cord. Leaving a 2½-inch tail, begin 3 inches below the top, concealing the tail as you wrap. Use a needle to pull the yarn through the wrapping.

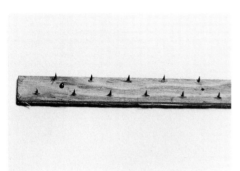

2: Tackless stripping, designed to hold wall-to-wall carpeting in place without visible tack heads, has short, protruding points that will grip the entire top edge of the wall hanging and hold it securely. Simply nail the molding to the wall and press the edge of the hanging onto the points.

the wool, forming a 2-inch-long coil; then secure the cord by passing it through the coil (Figure E). Trim the ends of the cord close to the wrapping.

When all the tassels are made, the hanging is ready to be displayed. The best way to do this is to hang it on so-called tackless stripping (photograph 2). Nail the molding to the wall at the proper height, and simply press the top hem of the hanging onto it, being careful not to prick your hands on the sharp points. The points will grip the fabric and hold the hanging securely.

Needlecrafts
Rya rippled pillow $ ☒ ♟ ⚛

Short and long pile give the striped pillow pictured on page 1824 its sculptured look. Using wool yarn of two different weights adds to the texture. To make the pillow, you will need: a 17-inch-wide piece of rya backing fabric, ½ yard long. You can use any colors you like, of course, but to make the pillow shown, you will need yarn in the following colors and amounts: using wool yarn in 3.6-ounce, 160-yard skeins, 2½ skeins of rust (color 1) and 1 skein of brown (color 2); using wool rug yarn in 3.6-ounce, 130-yard skeins, 1 skein of beige (color 3). You will also need: a No. 13 tapestry needle; a 17-inch-square piece of heavy fabric in a color harmonious with the yarns (for the back of the pillow); sewing machine (optional); sewing needle; sewing thread matching the fabric used for the back of the pillow; straight pins; and scissors. For the inner pillow, you will need two 17-inch squares of muslin or other inexpensive lightweight fabric and polyester fiber for stuffing.

The Pillow Top
To prepare the yarn for the pillow top, untwist each skein and cut through it once where it is tied, forming 56-inch-long strands. To keep the top and bottom edges of the rya backing from raveling, turn them under ½ inch and baste in place.

Using the rya knot (see Craftnotes, page 1831) make the pillow top. Refer to the chart in Figure F for the yarn color, the number of strands of yarn to be threaded into the needle, and the length of the loops in each row. Since the beige yarn is of a heavier weight, and therefore a bit thicker than the other two, only three strands of it are used in the needle at one time. Begin knotting in the second row of openwork from the bottom of the rya backing fabric; begin and end each row in the fourth space in from the selvage at the sides. Cut each row of loops before going on to make the next row.

Row	Color	Strands	Loop (inches)	Row	Color	Strands	Loop (inches)
1	1	4	1	15	1	4	1
2	1	4	1	16	1	4	1
3	2	4	1	17	1	4	1
4	2 and 3	2 each	½	18	3	3	½
5	3	3	½	19	3	3	½
6	1	4	1	20	3	3	½
7	1	4	1	21	1	4	1
8	1	4	1	22	1	4	1
9	3	3	½	23	1	4	1
10	3	3	½	24	3	3	½
11	3	3	½	25	2 and 3	2 each	½
12	1	4	1	26	2	4	1
13	1	4	1	27	1	4	1
14	1	4	1	28	1	4	1

F

Figure F: Follow this chart when you make the rippled rya pillow cover pictured on page 1824. Refer to the chart each time you start a new row of knotting. Row 1 begins at the bottom left of the backing fabric if you are right-handed, the bottom right if you are left-handed.

Finishing

When the pillow top has been completed, make the inner pillow. Place the pieces of muslin together, edges even. Sew them together all around, making ½-inch seams and leaving a 4-inch opening on one side. Turn the inner pillow right side out and stuff it fully with polyester fiber. Fold the raw edges of the opening to the inside, and sew them together by hand.

To assemble the outer pillow (Figure G), place the rya pillow top and the fabric back together, edges even with right sides facing. Baste them together all around, about ¼ inch outside the rya knots. Make sure that none of the yarn has been caught in the basting. Stitch over the basting by hand or by machine, leaving an 8-inch opening on one side. Turn the pillow right side out and insert the inner pillow. Turn the raw edges of the pillow cover to the inside, and hand sew them together with tiny stitches.

Needlecrafts
Diamonds within a diamond $ ☒ ♙ 🧵

Using jute *aida* as a backing fabric, as was done in the diamond-decorated pillow pictured on page 1824, saves money and lets you combine embroidery or needlepoint stitches with rya loops. You can follow these directions for making this pillow, or, if you are an experienced needleworker, you can use this idea and design your own rya stitchery.

Materials

To make a 16-inch-square pillow (finished size), use an 18-inch-square piece of jute *aida* with a mesh of approximately four holes per inch. For the needlepoint center, use a No. 13 tapestry needle and heavy wool rug yarn in a light and dark shade of the same color (here, grayish olive); you will need about 10 yards of each shade. For the rya knots, you use the same needle; you need a total of about 600 yards of heavy wool yarn in four shades of one color. For the pillow pictured, yarn in the following colors and amounts was used: one-ply cowhair-and-wool yarn in pink, two 3.6-ounce, 160-yard skeins; three-ply Persian-type wool yarn in rust, peach, and deep rose, one-half 3.6-ounce, 130-yard skein of each. Additional supplies needed are: a waterproof marker; ruler; scissors; sewing needle; sewing machine (optional); 18-inch-square piece of heavy fabric in a color harmonious with the yarns used (for the back of the outer pillow); and sewing thread to match the heavy fabric. To make the inner pillow, you need two pieces of 17-inch-square muslin (or other inexpensive, lightweight fabric) and polyester fiber for stuffing.

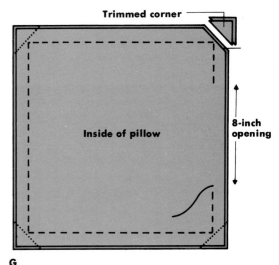

G

Figure G: With right sides facing, sew the rya pillow top to the fabric back. Sew along three sides and all four corners, leaving an 8-inch opening along one side. Trim the corners to within ¼ inch of the knots to reduce bulk; then turn the pillow cover right side out.

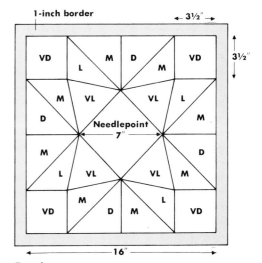

Tone key

VD: very dark   **L: light**
D: dark   **VL: very light**
M: medium

H

Figure H: Following the dimensions and color suggestions given in this diagram for the needlepoint-rya pillow (pictured on page 1824), mark the pattern on the jute *aida*. The sections are filled with light-to-dark combinations of yarn to obtain the effect of a pinwheel in motion. The center diamond shape is to be filled with needlepoint stitches, following the chart in Figure I, page 1830.

The center of the jute-backed pillow cover is worked in vertical needlepoint stitches. In order to make sure the stitches hide the jute fabric over which they are worked, thread the tapestry needle with two strands of yarn.

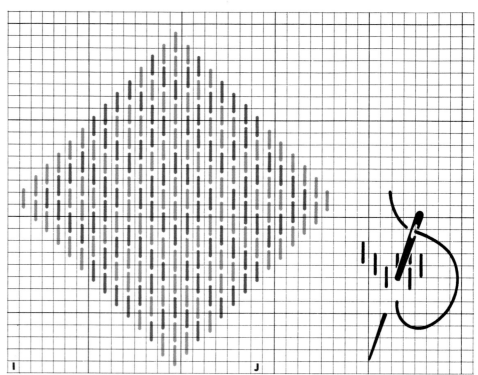

Figure I: This chart shows where the vertical bargello stitches of needlepoint are placed within the 7-inch diamond-shaped area at the center of the pillow. How the bargello stitch is made is shown in Figure J.

Figure J: To work the bargello needlepoint stitches, take vertical stitches over two threads of the jute fabric as shown above. The top of one stitch shares a hole with the bottom of the stitch directly above it.

Needlepointing

By hand or by machine, stitch all around the jute *aida* backing close to the edge to keep it from raveling as you work. With ruler and waterproof marker, draw a pattern for the design (Figure H, page 1829) on the backing. Following the chart in Figure I, work the needlepoint section first. The photograph, left, shows a close-up of this section. In the chart, the blue horizontal and vertical lines represent the horizontal and vertical threads of the jute. The needlepoint stitches are indicated in light and dark green to correspond to the colors of the yarn used to make them. In this type of needlepoint, called bargello, every stitch is vertical and is worked over two horizontal threads of jute (Figure J). To begin, cut the needlepoint yarn into 18-inch lengths, and thread the tapestry needle with two strands (see Craftnotes opposite). Start stitching at the top of the outlined diamond-shaped area, using the darker yarn. First work the seven small diamond motifs and the two partial diamond motifs at the top and bottom points. Then fill in the rows between them with the lighter-colored yarn. Finally, fill in the light-colored centers of the diamonds. When beginning and ending a length of yarn, catch the end under other stitches on the underside of the jute.

Rya Knotting

Untwist each skein of heavy wool yarn and cut through it once where it is tied, forming strands of equal length. Thread the tapestry needle with four strands of yarn and work rya knots in every other row (see Craftnotes opposite). Starting at the bottom left-hand corner of the pillow top, make the loops 1 inch long. Cut most of them as you finish each row but leave some uncut for extra textural interest. You can use the diagram in Figure H, page 1829, as a general guide in placing the yarn colors; these should appear to be mixed at random, giving a dappled, confetti look. To get this effect, for the very light areas use four strands of pink in the needle; for the light areas, use two strands each of peach and pink; for the medium areas use three strands of peach and one strand of rust; for the dark areas use three strands of rust and one strand of rose; and for the very dark areas use three strands of rose and one strand of rust.

Finishing

To finish the pillow, assemble the outer pillow and the inner pillow by following the directions given for the rippled pillow on page 1829.

CRAFTNOTES: MAKING RYA KNOTS ON A WOVEN BACKING

The knot used for rya is also called a ghiordes knot; three or four strands of yarn are threaded through a large, blunt tapestry needle and are twisted around the yarns of the backing fabric. Thus, they are not really knotted in the sense of being tied; they are held in place by tension only, and in effect are embroidered on the backing fabric.

Cut the three or four strands the same length (about 5 feet); they will be treated as a single unit throughout. To thread each unit of strands, fold a 1- or 2-inch end of the yarn over the needle and pull it taut (above, left). Pinch the fold with thumb and forefinger and slide the thread off the needle. Push the pinched fold through the eye of the needle (above, right).

Knotting on rya backing

With selvages (the tightly woven finished edges) at the sides, begin knotting at the lower left-hand corner of the backing fabric. The knots are worked across, from left to right, in the openwork rows of the backing. (If you are left-handed, begin at the lower right-hand corner, and work from right to left.) The exposed sets of three vertical threads in the backing are treated as single threads. Work each knot over two adjacent sets of threads, and work across the entire row before starting the next row above it.

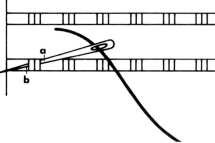

To begin, insert the needle at point **a** and come up at point **b**, going under the first set of threads from right to left (above). Pull the yarn through, leaving a tail as long as the rya loops will be. Hold this end below the row with your thumb.

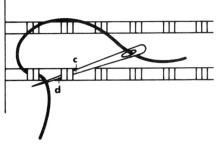

With the yarn lying above the row, insert the needle at point **c** and come up at point **d**, going under the next set of threads from right to left. Pull the yarn through and tighten it to complete the first knot.

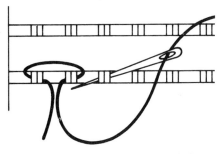

To begin the next knot, hold the yarn below the row. As before, insert the needle from right to left under the next set of threads. Pull the yarn through, leaving a loop of the wanted length. Continue knotting, either making all loops approximately the same length or varying the length for a shaggy effect.

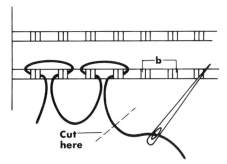

When you come to the end of a row, cut the yarn the length of the loops after completing the last knot. If you want to cut the pile loops, do so for an entire row at one time, as soon as you finish that row. To change colors within a row, work across the row to the color change and cut the yarn (above). Start the new color as in the first step, going under the next set of threads (**b** in the drawing).

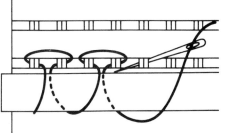

After you make the first knot, you may want to use a ruler, wooden stick, or strip of cardboard as wide as the height of the loops planned so you can keep the pile uniform. Bring the yarn under the stick to begin each new loop, then over it to complete the loop. Slide the stick to the right as the work proceeds.

Knotting on jute aida

Making knots on jute **aida** is basically the same as making them on the rya backing. Unless you want a very dense pile, skip every other row of the jute as you knot. In this way, you will maintain a ½-inch space between rows. The holes in jute **aida** are spaced somewhat farther apart than are the holes in rya backing, so you will be making fewer knots per row and will need less yarn to finish a project.

Maggie Quitko began this Impressionist-style rya rug with only the barest of design ideas in mind. Following her suggestions below, you can design your own rya rug, pillow, or wall hanging, using her approach.

Needlecrafts
Design an original rya

You can design your own rya rug, wall hanging, or pillow if you like. There are thousands of design ideas—modern and traditional, realistic and abstract—that you can readily adapt to knotted rya pile.

Materials
To design your own rya, you will need the following supplies: pencil; ruler; plain sketching paper; waterproof felt-tipped pens; acrylic or oil paints and paint-brushes; and a sheet of plain paper the size the finished rya is to be. Depending on the design method used, you will also need carbon paper, dressmaker's transfer paper or a hot-iron transfer pencil (available at needlecraft shops), and an iron. To make the rya you will need: prewoven rya backing or jute *aida;* rya and other types of yarn (the guidelines that follow will help you determine the size of the backing and amount of yarn needed); scissors; No. 13 tapestry needle; sewing needle; and sewing thread in off-white or beige.

Choosing Designs and Colors
Design ideas can be found everywhere—in museums, art galleries, books, magazines, and in the everyday objects that surround you. Deciding to take a design from nature is a perfect excuse for a leisurely trek through the woods or a field of flowers. If you wish to compose a bold geometric design, a compass and ruler will be invaluable. A free-form design, such as the one used in the rug pictured above, can begin as only a few curved lines. Simply pick up a pencil, crayon, or pen and start doodling. Let your imagination do the work; make random swirls, flowing curves, and fluid lines. When you arrive at a basic design that appeals to you, add some smaller areas and fill in the shapes with color. Above all, keep the design simple, since the shaggy rya pile tends to blur (and sometimes obliterate) small design details. Good rya designs stem from a pleasing combination of yarn textures, colors, and patterns.

When you choose the colors for your rya, keep in mind the area where it will be used or displayed. This is not to suggest that you duplicate the color scheme of a room; that would be dull and probably impossible. Simply make sure the colors you choose will be harmonious with the colors already in the room.

Estimating Yarn Needs

If you take your design to the yarn shop, someone there may be able to help you estimate the amount of yarn you will need. To estimate the yarn needs yourself, use this procedure to determine the total number of yards needed: Double the desired length of the pile and then add ½ inch—this gives the amount of yarn needed for each knot. Multiply this figure by the number of knots in one row (three and one-half per inch for rya backing, two per inch for the jute *aida*) and by how many strands will be threaded in the needle at one time (usually three or four). This will give you the amount of yarn needed for one row of knots. Multiply this amount by the number of rows of knots (usually one every ½ inch for either type of backing). This will give you the total number of inches of yarn needed. Divide this total by 36 to convert the number to yards.

The rug pictured measures 37 by 52 inches, was made on rya backing, and has a 2-inch-long pile. Using the method described, a total of 60,372 inches or 1,677 yards of yarn were needed to make the rug. To determine how much yarn of each color you will need, you must approximate the proportion of the rya that will be worked in each color, and buy that portion of the total yardage in that color. For example, if you need a total of 800 yards of yarn, and approximately one-fourth of your design is red, you will need to buy 200 yards of red yarn.

When you are ready to buy yarn, don't expect the colors to match the colors in your sketch exactly. At this point, be flexible enough to be able to change your color plan slightly. Pick out skeins of yarn in the colors closest to those you had in mind, and see how they look together. The difference may be so slight that it doesn't matter, or the difference may make the colors even more appealing to you. You might even be so caught up in the beauty of the colors available that you will change your plan entirely in order to use the colors you like the best.

Much of the beauty of ryas stems from the fact that a single color area gains greater depth and intensity if it includes several shades of one color. So buy yarns in different but closely related shades of your design colors, and when you begin work on a color area, thread a mixture (usually three or four strands) of slightly different shades in the needle (see Craftnotes, page 1831). Another way to add richness to the color and texture of your rya is to combine different types of yarn in the design. On page 1825 you will find a discussion of the various yarns suitable for ryas, as in the pillows (page 1824) and the cat (page 1834).

Backing Fabrics

The characteristics of the two kinds of backing fabric—special rya backing or jute *aida*—are discussed on page 1826. Allow a generous 2½ inches extra on each edge if it will be finished by hemming, as on a rug or wall hanging; 1 inch extra on each edge is sufficient if it will be seamed, as in a pillow. If you are using rya backing for a rug or wall hanging, try to purchase backing that is the same width you want your finished piece to be. The tightly woven selvage will form finished edges on the sides, eliminating the need for side hems.

Making the Rya

To begin your rya, you must put a design on the backing. With practice, you may be able to paint the design directly on the backing freehand. A safer method is to make a small sketch of your design, then when it satisfies you, enlarge it onto a sheet of paper to make a full-sized pattern for the finished piece.

To enlarge the sketch, follow the grid method. With pencil and ruler, draw a grid over your small sketch. Make ¼-, ½-, ¾-, or 1-inch squares, depending on how complicated your design is and how much you need to enlarge it. Your sketch will bear a resemblance to Figure B, page 1827. On a sheet of paper large enough for a full-sized pattern, make an equal number of larger squares to correspond to the smaller squares on your sketch. For example, if your sketch is 8 inches wide and has ½-inch squares, and you want to enlarge the design to 16 inches wide, make the second set of squares 1 inch. Then transfer your design to the larger paper by copying the lines of the sketch, one square at a time.

There are three ways to transfer your full-sized pattern to the backing. If you have large, simple shapes, simply cut out the pattern pieces along the design lines, and trace around their edges with a waterproof felt-tipped pen. For a more complex design, place dressmaker's transfer paper, carbon side down, over the backing. Put the pattern, face up, over this and pin or tape it in place. Then go over the lines of the design with a pencil or dressmaker's tracing wheel. The third method requires the use of a hot-iron transfer pencil, the kind used by embroiderers to transfer designs to fabric. Place the pattern, face down, against a window pane so the design shows through. Go over the lines of the design with the transfer pencil. Pin or tape the pattern, transfer-pencil side down, on the backing. Set your iron at a low temperature, and apply it to the pattern with a stamping motion, so the image will not smudge. Lift a corner of the pattern to see if the design has been transferred satisfactorily before you remove the pattern.

At this point, you may want to indicate the colors of the design. You can use broad-tipped waterproof pens, acrylics, or paint to do this. If the design is simple, you can use the small color sketch as a guide as you knot.

Knotting
Once the design has been transferred to the backing, you are ready to begin knotting the yarn in place. Follow the procedures described in the earlier projects, not only for knotting (Craftnotes, page 1831) but for hemming (page 1826) and displaying (page 1828) a wall hanging (a rug is hemmed the same way but you can sew rug binding over the edge of the hem if you wish), or for finishing a pillow (page 1829). If you are using one type of yarn, open up each skein and cut through it once, forming strands of equal length. If you are using different types of yarn and plan to combine them in the needle, measure and cut each type into equal lengths. Note that not all yarns are skeined the same.

Shown here are some of the yarns used to make the pile of the rya cat. Starting at the top, the yarns and the amounts needed are: Swedish rya rug yarn in burnt orange (two 3.6-ounce skeins); Swedish rug wool in medium yellow-orange (two 3.6-ounce skeins); orange and yellow space-dyed brushed wool (two 2-ounce skeins); red-orange single-ply cowhair-and-wool yarn (one 3.6-ounce skein); Swedish rya rug yarn in pale yellow (one quarter of a 3.6-ounce skein); Donegal tweed wool in dark brown (one 4-ounce skein); Donegal tweed wool in honey (one 4-ounce skein). Not shown are: Swedish rya rug yarn in light yellow-orange (one 3.6-ounce skein); and light orange mohair (one 1¾-ounce skein).

Weaving, Knotting, Braiding
Woven rya cat

A flat, plush, nontraditional rya cat was made with the traditional rya technique of weaving on a loom. Many different yarns, including mohair, rug wool, Donegal tweed wool, and brushed wool, were used. The front and back were woven and knotted separately, then sewn together and stuffed. An oval felt bottom makes a stable base for the cat, which can be used as a toy or a pillow.

When rya rugs are made on a loom in the traditional method, the rya backing and the pile are woven and knotted simultaneously. A loom was used to make the rya cat pictured opposite. Its shape and the different colors of pile were obtained by following a pattern taped to the loom frame under the warp (the lengthwise threads). Since only a plain weave (with crosswise threads going over and under lengthwise threads in alternating rows) is needed for the backing, a frame loom, one of the simplest of all looms, can be used. If you are an experienced weaver, you can easily adapt the directions to suit a more elaborate table or floor loom.

Materials

To make a frame loom, use artist's canvas-stretcher strips, sold in art supply stores. Buy a pair of 32-inch-long strips and a pair of 40-inch-long strips. (The finished weaving measures 18 by 26 inches, but to allow the extra space needed during the weaving process, the outside measurement of the loom should be at least 32 by 40 inches.) You will also need: a 28-by-38-inch sheet of paper for the pattern; ruler; pencil; black felt-tipped pen; 50 yards of string (for heddles, Figure L); two dowels each about 44 inches long (for heddle rods); scissors; staple gun and staples; 100 yards of heavy yarn or string (for the heading); a beater such as a table fork, comb, or stick beater (to push the crosswise threads in place); a 24-inch-long shuttle (for carrying the crosswise threads); 1½ pounds of polyester fiber for stuffing; and a 5½-by-26-inch piece of orange felt. You will also need some orange sewing thread; a sewing needle; large needle such as a tapestry needle; three buttons (for eyes and nose); 2 yards of wide satin ribbon; and six broom straws (for whiskers). For the plain weaving, these types and amounts of yarn were used: 270 yards of cotton warp in orange (for the lengthwise threads) and 11 ounces of light- to medium-weight wool yarn in orange (for the crosswise threads). For the rya pile, a total of about 35 ounces of nine different yarns of various types, weights, and shades of orange were used. The pile yarns and the amounts used are listed under the photograph opposite, left. All the yarns, or similar ones, are available at large yarn shops and weaving supply shops. You may not be able to duplicate all the yarns, but if you try to approximate the tones of the different combinations, they will distinguish the light and dark areas of the design.

Making and Warping the Frame

To begin, assemble the frame by interlocking the corners of the stretcher strips. Make sure the corners form right angles; then staple the joints to stabilize them.

Weaving is the process of interlacing two sets of threads at right angles to form a web. One set of threads (the lengthwise threads, called the warp) remains stationary so the second set of threads (the crosswise threads, called the weft or the filler) can be woven through. The warp for this rya, 32 inches long, covers an area 27 inches wide. (The weaving process will pull the warp threads toward the center causing the weaving to shrink about 2 inches; so 2 inches have been added to the finished width sought.) On a frame loom, one continuous warp strand is wound around the top and bottom strip in figure eights (Figure K). Form a total of 140 warp threads—five per inch. To space the warp threads, use a ruler and pencil to divide the center 28 inches of the top and bottom strips into inches.

Heddle Rods and Shuttle

To make it easier to pass the weft (crosswise) threads over and under the fixed warp threads, a device called a heddle rod is used to pick up a set of alternate threads as a single unit. You could pick up every other thread, one by one, with your fingers, but that would be a tedious task. Instead, to raise all the alternate threads at one time, a string (called a heddle) is looped under each alternate thread and over a dowel (called a heddle rod) as shown in Figure L. When a set of alternate threads has been looped, the dowel is lifted and the threads are raised. This forms an opening called a shed through which the weft thread is passed. In order for the weave to interlock, you now need to form a second shed by lowering the upper threads and raising the bottom threads; so you need a second heddle rod looped with string. The weft is passed back through this second shed; so the crosswise thread passes under the lengthwise threads that it passed over in the first instance, and over those it passed under.

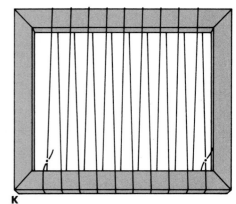

K

Figure K: To warp a frame loom—that is, to place the stationary lengthwise threads—knot the warp thread around the bottom strip at the left corner. Then start winding by bringing it to the top, over the front of the top strip and to the back, down and over the bottom front, and around to the back, in a figure eight configuration. Continue until you have a total of 140 such warp threads, spaced about five to the inch. The drawing shows only a few warp threads for clarity. Fasten off the end with another knot.

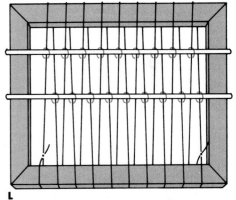

L

Figure L: Heddle rods and strings raise or lower alternate warp threads as a unit so crosswise threads can easily be passed through the sheds (openings) thus formed. To make the heddles, cut a 6-inch length of string for each warp thread. Place a heddle dowel across the loom frame near one end of the warp threads, and put a ruler or stick next to it as a spacer. Working with the top set of warp threads only, loop string around the dowel and ruler and under the warp thread. Tie the ends of the string around the dowel and trim close to the knot. Continue tying strings around the ruler and the rod, catching the next warp thread on top, until all the top warps have been tied. Then pull out the ruler, leaving loops of uniform size. To make the second shed, repeat the process with the second dowel and the second set of threads at the other end of the loom.

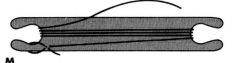

M

Figure M: To wind yarn around the shuttle, tie a loop at one end of the yarn and catch the loop on one of the shuttle's prongs. Then wrap the yarn snugly from end to end so it lies between the notches of the shuttle.

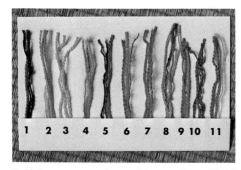

3: Make your own color card to organize and label the various combinations of yarns used in the rya knots of the cat. Cut short lengths of the different yarns that make up each combination, and tape each group to a piece of stiff paper. Assign each group a number from 1 to 11, arranging them so they correspond in tone to those shown in the photograph. (For instance, No. 1 is the darkest combination pictured, No. 3 is the lightest in tone.) The combinations shown above consist of:

1: One strand of burnt orange rug yarn, two strands of brown Donegal tweed wool.

2: One strand each of light yellow-orange rug yarn, medium yellow-orange rug yarn, and light orange mohair.

3: Three strands of pale yellow rug yarn.

4: One strand each of light yellow-orange rug yarn, medium yellow-orange rug yarn, and orange brushed wool.

5: One strand each of burnt orange rug yarn, brown Donegal tweed wool, and honey Donegal tweed wool.

6: One strand each of medium yellow-orange rug yarn, burnt orange rug yarn, and orange brushed wool.

7: One strand each of burnt orange rug yarn, orange brushed wool, and orange cowhair-and-wool single-ply yarn.

8: One strand each of light yellow-orange rug yarn, medium yellow-orange rug yarn, honey Donegal tweed wool, and orange cowhair-and-wool single-ply yarn.

9: One strand each of medium yellow-orange rug yarn, burnt orange rug yarn, and orange cowhair-and-wool yarn.

10: One strand of burnt orange rug yarn, two strands of honey Donegal tweed wool.

11: One strand of orange mohair, two strands of burnt orange rug wool.

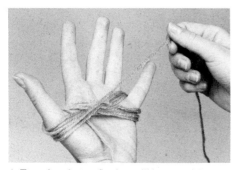

4: To make a butterfly that will let you make rya knots on a loom without tangling the yarn, wrap the yarns to be used in the design color combination around your thumb and little finger in figure eights. For clarity, only one strand of yarn is being wrapped in the photograph, but you can do the same with three or four as needed.

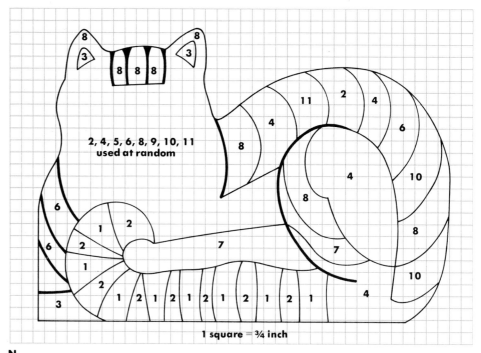

2, 4, 5, 6, 8, 9, 10, 11 used at random

1 square = ¾ inch

N

Figure N: To enlarge the design for the rya cat, use a pencil and ruler to draw a ¾-inch grid on a 28-by-38-inch sheet of paper. Then copy the design, square by square, onto the larger grid. Transfer the numbers onto the pattern; they are the key to the numbered combinations of yarn used (see photograph 3). The heavy black lines in the pattern are worked in the darkest combination of yarns (No. 1).

To facilitate passing the crosswise thread back and forth, it is wrapped on a long, thin, flat stick called a shuttle (Figure M, page 1835). You can buy a 24-inch-long shuttle from a weaving supply store, or make one from ⅛- or ¼-inch thick wood or hardboard. Cut out a notch at each end and sand the edges smooth.

Getting Ready

Enlarge the pattern for the cat (Figure N) and go over the lines with a black felt-tipped pen so they will be clearly visible when the pattern is placed under the warp threads. Number the areas, as is done on the pattern, so you can use the coded color chart (photograph 3) as a guide.

Each rya knot is made with three or four different threads simultaneously; because each knot blends different colors, a subtle shading effect is achieved. Make a color card of the different combinations of yarns to guide you (photograph 3). If you create your own color combinations, have some that are definitely dark (like No. 1 and No. 5), and some that are light (No. 2 and No. 3); number them to correspond to the light and dark combinations shown in the photograph of the color card. This way, you can follow the numbers in the pattern even if you use a different color combination. When the color card is complete, use it as a guide to wind the butterflies (photograph 4) that you will use for making rya knots.

Weaving

To space the ends of the warp threads properly, weave a 2-inch heading of plain weave, using heavy string or yarn. To weave plain weave, wind string or heavy yarn around the shuttle and pass the shuttle through alternate sheds. Each time you pass a crosswise thread through, beat it down (push it snugly into place) with a table fork, comb, or stick. To begin and end the yarn, tuck a 2-inch tail back into the weaving at the sides (selvages).

Next, wind the weft yarn around the shuttle, and work back and forth in plain weave for another 1½ inches; do not pull the weft taut when you pass it through the warp. Beat the weft down firmly after every row. Place the enlarged pattern under the warp and tape it to the sides of the frame. The bottom of the pattern should be lined up with the top row of completed weaving. Put in the first row of rya knots, working from left to right and making each knot over two warp threads. The knots

5: To begin making a rya knot on a loom, pick up the warp thread and pass the butterfly from right to left under it. Leave an end of yarn behind as long as the pile will be.

6: To finish forming the knot, lay the yarn above the row. Then pick up the next warp thread to the right, and pass the butterfly under this thread, again from right to left.

7: Hold the end in place and pull the yarn, tightening the knot and leaving a loop as high as the pile. For the next knot, repeat from photograph 5, making the knot over the next two warp threads.

are made as shown in the Craftnotes, page 1831, except that a needle is not used; how they are made on a loom is shown in photographs 5 through 9. Use the different combinations of yarn colors indicated by the numbers on the pattern. When you make the knots, form loops 1¼ to 1½ inches long. After your first row of knots is completed, work in plain weave with the weft yarn for a little more than ½ inch (it will be compressed to ½ inch after the next row of knots is completed). Continue weaving and knotting in this way, alternating every row of rya knots with a bit more than ½ inch of plain weave. Follow the outline of the pattern to get the shape of the cat (photograph 10). To do this, skip the warp threads outside the pattern while knotting as the shape narrows.

When the knotting of the cat has been completed, remove it from the loom by cutting the warp threads at top and bottom. Leave at least 6 inches of warp threads extending from the cat's ears and back. Tie these warp ends together in pairs and set the front of the cat aside. To make a pattern for the back of the cat, place the pattern you already have face down on a window pane so the outline shows through. Go over the outline of the pattern, omitting internal lines and numbers, to get a reversed pattern.

To weave the back of the cat, rewarp the loom, set up the heddle rods, and follow the same technique you used to weave the front of the cat. But use combination No. 6 throughout for the rya knots, putting in only random knots of other combinations until they are used up. Cut the cat back from the loom, again leaving at least 6 inches of warp threads extending from the ears. Tie the pairs of warp threads.

Finishing

Sew on the buttons for the cat's eyes and nose. Put the front and back pieces of the cat together on a flat surface, rya sides facing and edges matching. Tie each loose pair of warp ends of one piece to the corresponding ends of the other piece. Tie the knots tightly so the edges of the weavings are brought close together. The ends will not always match exactly; so occasionally you will need to thread one end in a tapestry needle and work it through the edge of the woven fabric until it reaches its partner.

When all the loose ends have been tied (leave the bottom open), trim them to about 1 inch long. Then thread the tapestry needle with a double strand of warp thread, and sew around the top and sides of the cat, catching just a few threads of the weaving along the edges. Turn the cat right side out and stuff it with the polyester fiber. Pull out the string or heavy yarn heading that was used for spacing, and tie adjacent warp ends, thus freed, in pairs. Shape the rectangle of felt into an oval by trimming the 5½-inch-wide ends to 2½ inches. With a sewing needle and thread, sew the felt to the bottom of the cat. To do this, set the felt into the opening at the bottom, over the stuffing. As you sew with tiny stitches, turn the 1½-inch band of weaving of the cat and a ¾-inch band of felt to the inside. Tie the ribbon around the cat's neck and make a big floppy bow. Insert three broom straws on each side of the nose, forming the whiskers.

For related entries, see "Florentine Stitch," "Hooked Rugs," "Tablet and Frame Weaving."

8: To change colors, cut the yarn, leaving an end the same length as the pile. Begin the next color combination over the next two warp threads.

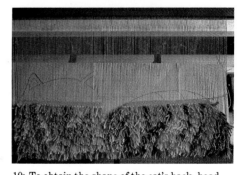

9: To make sure you cut all of the loops at their bottoms, cut them as you go along each time you change to a new color combination.

10: To obtain the shape of the cat's back, head, and ears, follow the outline of the pattern in making rya knots and weaving. As you weave, simply skip the warp ends beyond the edges of the shape.

SAIL MAKING AND REPAIR
The Original Wind Machine

David Noyes grew up sailing on Long Island Sound, and in 1972, while a student at Yale, he was selected an All-American sailor by the Intercollegiate Yacht Racing Association of North America. He makes sails as a hobby and is currently working on a set of sails for a boat he will use in competition trials for the 1976 Olympics. David is a free-lance journalist and a former editor with Sail *magazine.*

Early Egyptian ships used three-cornered fore-and-aft sails to work their way up the Nile.

The Norsemen preferred square sails for their galleys but needed oars to move into the wind.

Sail makers have always agreed on one thing: Sail power is a wonderful way to use energy without consuming it. Beyond that, there has been little agreement over the years, even on such a basic question as which type of sail is best. About 2000 years ago Egyptians used three-cornered sails (top, left) to propel their boats up the Nile after floating downstream. But the Phoenicians, Greeks, and Norsemen who followed them preferred square sails with four corners (bottom, left).

Three-cornered sails are usually known as fore-and-aft sails because they are aligned with the length (the keel line) of a ship. Square sails usually line up at right angles to the keel; they can be rotated around the mast but the wind must push on the back of a square sail to move the ship. By contrast, the flow of air across a fore-and-aft sail provides the forward push, and these sails can be swung to either side to take advantage of wind from every direction except head on.

Square sails dominated ocean sailing for about 200 years, reaching a peak of popularity in the 1800s, when huge ships carrying three to five masts and 15 to 30 square sails plied the ocean trade routes (below, left). But even in this period, fore-and-aft sails were not forgotten. The Arabian dhow, a two-masted descendant of the Egyptian barge, still used them to sail along the Mediterranean coastline and in the Indian Ocean. Indonesian sailors also used three-cornered sails on their speedy praus (or proas), with an outrigger at the side to improve the balance (below, center). One of the ships Columbus used on his 1492 voyage to America—the caravel *Niña*—used three-cornered sails in a three-masted arrangement similar to that shown below, right. Later, three-cornered sails appeared between the masts of square-rigged ships and as triangular staysails (so-called because they were located on the stays—the rope braces running from the forward mast to the ship's bowsprit on the bow). These staysails were the forerunners of today's jib sails that mount in front of the mainsail's mast.

After 1860, American shipbuilders largely abandoned square sails and adopted fore-and-aft sails rigged on several masts. The number of masts increased from three to four to six, reaching a record of seven on the schooner Thomas W. Lawson built in 1902. What the resourceful Yankee shipbuilders were seeking was more speed and maneuverability, which they could get from fore-and-aft sails whose front edges were fully supported by masts but which were free to move from side to side, as if they were hinged to the masts. They also found that these new rigs were safer. Rather than shivering or even slamming back like a square sail when the ship headed too close to the direction the wind was coming from, the fore-and-aft sails could be released so they merely flapped harmlessly from side to side.

Opposite: A small triangular sail can propel a small dinghy briskly in light winds.

Square-rigged ships sometimes carried three-cornered sails up front and between the rows of square sails.

Indonesian praus have a triangular fore-and-aft sail, and an outrigger to help maintain balance.

This fifteenth century caravel, like the *Niña* that sailed with Columbus, used three-cornered sails.

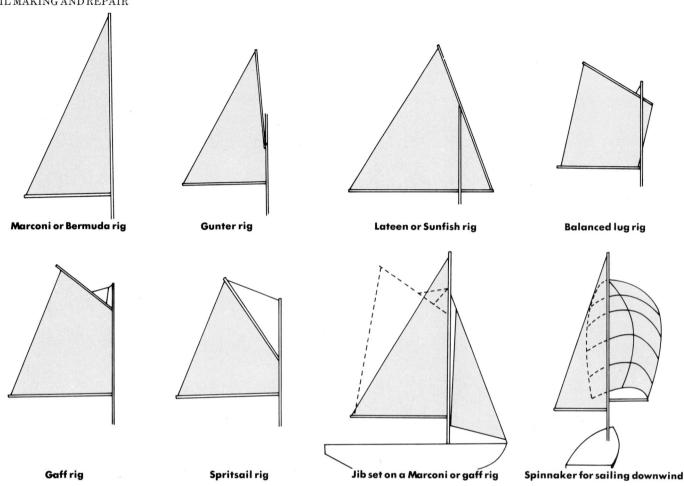

Marconi or Bermuda rig   **Gunter rig**   **Lateen or Sunfish rig**   **Balanced lug rig**

Gaff rig   **Spritsail rig**   **Jib set on a Marconi or gaff rig**   **Spinnaker for sailing downwind**

A

Figure A: Sailing rigs for dinghies come in a great variety of shapes, as these examples suggest.

Today's smaller sailboats have, of course, far fewer masts than the large schooners of the late 1800s. But all of them use fore-and-aft sails, from tiny Sunfish to the lofty America's Cup defenders in the 12-meter class. Sizes vary to suit the size of the boat and, as Figure A shows, so do the shapes. Although the triangular Marconi rig (color photo, page 1839) is probably the most popular, four-sided fore-and-aft sails are also widely used.

All of these rigs share the quality inherent in fore-and-aft sails—the ability to let the boat sail close to the direction the wind is coming from. To understand how they can do this, think of the sail as a curved shape—like an airplane wing standing on end. The wind striking the sail's front edge is split so that one part travels around the outside of the curve and the other part travels across the inside of the curve (Figure B). The air traveling the longer distance, around the outside, must travel faster to reach the back edge of the curve at the same time as the air taking a short-cut across the inside. As the speed of the air going around the outside increases, the pressure it exerts on the outside of the sail decreases, becoming weaker than the pressure of the slower-moving air traveling across the inside. The result is a force exerted against the sail from the inside. Acting alone, this force would tend to push the boat sideways. But when the hull is designed to move forward rather than sideways (on some boats a keel or centerboard also helps to resist side slipping), the sideways push is converted into a thrust that moves the boat forward against the wind.

The trick in designing a sail that will move a boat into the wind is to make it in such a way that it can hold a curved shape when mounted on the mast. The sail's outline is not of key importance—it can be either triangular or four-sided. But the cross-sectional shape from the front (leading) edge to the back (trailing) edge must have the deepest part of the curve in the front 40 percent of the sail for it to drive the boat forward efficiently.

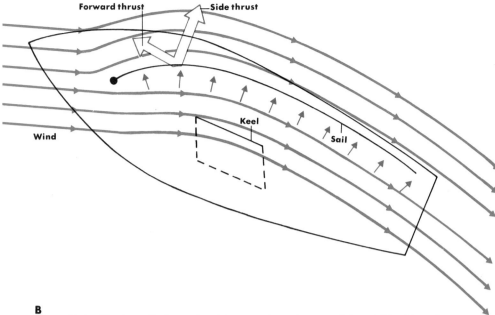

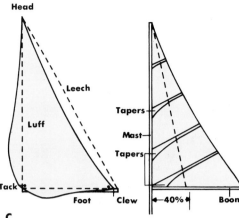

B
Figure B: A sailboat gets its forward push because air moving around the outside of the sail must travel faster to reach the back of the sail at the same time as the air taking a shortcut across the inside. The faster moving air exerts less pressure on the sail than the slower moving air, creating a thrust (red arrows) that tries to push the boat sideways. But the resistance of the hull shape (and the keel, if there is one) converts the side thrust into a forward push.

C
Figure C: To make sure a sail can develop the curvature needed to propel a boat, extra material is added to its forward and bottom edges, as at left, above. In addition, small triangular tapers are cut from the forward 40 percent of the panels that make up the sail, as in the broad-seaming method shown at right, above, and described in the text.

In the days of the square riggers, sailors tried to rotate the square sails on the mast so that, depending on the wind's direction, sometimes one edge of the sail became the leading edge, sometimes the other. Since sails were braced only on the top and bottom, neither edge let the all-important curve develop from front to back to create a forward thrust. In modern mainsail rigs, the entire leading edge of the sail is supported by the mast from top to bottom. This permits the special curve to form from front to back, creating forward thrust. The Marconi sail that I will show you how to make for a dinghy (page 1844) is supported in this way.

But simply mounting the forward edge of a sail on a fixed mast will not assure the most desirable cross-sectional shape in the sail when the wind is blowing toward the boat. To make sure that curve will form, you must add a few extra inches of material in the belly of the sail by cutting the front and bottom edges in a convex curve (Figure C). Then, when the sail is attached to the vertical mast and the horizontal boom, the extra cloth will be pushed back and up, creating the curvature needed. This is called the luff curve method of introducing curvature.

To make doubly sure you get that curved shape, you can cut thin, tapered triangles out of the sail in small, measured amounts, widest near the mast, then sew the sections together—much as a dressmaker cuts clothes to shape them around body curves. This helps control the depth and location of the sail's curvature. This method—called broad seaming—is also shown in Figure C. Since the sail is assembled from several panels, broad seaming does not create extra seams. (These techniques for shaping a mainsail also apply to a jib sail, with the exceptions noted on page 1847.)

The sailcloth generally used today is a synthetic material made of Dacron fibers, stronger per unit of weight and more mildew-resistant than the cotton canvas that was once used. It is less likely to stretch out of shape than nylon sailcloth, which should be used only in sails for light breezes or for sailing with the wind. Dacron sailcloth is woven on special looms in a way that makes the cloth stay strong and taut along the lines of the threads (Figure D) although it is slightly elastic along the 45-degree bias. The cloth is treated with a special resin to add strength, uniformity, and stability.

Most sailcloth is delivered with selvage lines printed parallel to the length of the roll ½ inch in from the top and bottom edges. These lines are helpful guides when you want to sew a straight seam.

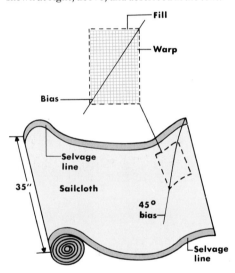

D
Figure D: Sailcloth comes in 35-inch wide rolls with selvage lines printed ½ inch in from each edge. A sail is made up of several panels of cloth (as in Figure C) for greater strength.

Sewing a seam

Sewing a good seam in a sail takes practice. You need to know your sewing machine, the tension of its thread, and the speed of its feeder. If you use a clear adhesive tape that is sticky on both sides to hold the seam as you sew, it will help you maintain equal tension on both pieces of cloth.

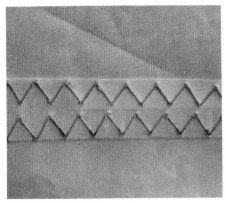

Keep lines of stitching parallel and move alongside the edges (above), but never over them.

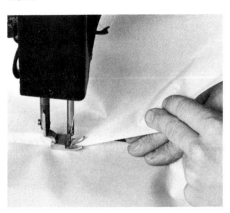

If you don't have double-sided sticky tape, maintain equal tension by crossing your hands so that your left hand is feeding the cloth on the right side of the seam and your right hand the cloth on the left (above).

Punching a grommet

To put a grommet (a small brass ring that holds a rope) into a sail, you need the grommet, a grommet hole cutter, die and inserting punch, and a wooden mallet. Hold the hole cutter in the exact location where you wish to mount the grommet, and hit it once or twice with the mallet. This will make a hole that is slightly smaller than the central cone of the grommet.

Force the cone half of the grommet through the hole. On the other side of the sailcloth, fit the washer half of the grommet over the nose of the protruding cone. Lay the top part of the grommet in the groove in the base. Fit the washer over the cone (above) and fit the spindle on top of that, with its guide resting in the hole of the cone.

Now hit it twice more with your mallet to ensure a secure hold on the cloth (above). Any more pounding might rip the cloth.

Repairing a small tear

A small tear in a sail can be hand-stitched, using a dressmaker's herringbone stitch.

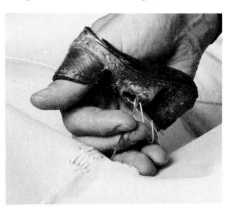

To do this, use medium-weight waxed polyester sewing thread, a sewing palm (above), and a No. 15 or 16 sewing needle, as above. Start by piercing the cloth about ¼ inch to the left of the tear with an upward stroke.

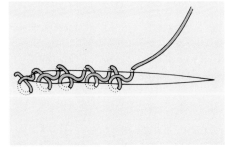

Cross over the tear and pierce downward. Now bring the needle up through the middle of the tear behind your first stitch (above). Pull the tear together smoothly but not too tightly as you pass over the stitch. Continue down through the tear and begin your second stitch on the left of the tear with an upward stroke. Repeat until the tear is closed.

MAKING AND REPAIRING SAILS

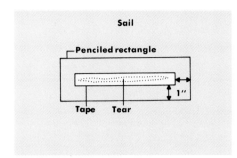

Repairing a large tear

Tape the tear together temporarily (above), applying about the same tension on both pieces of cloth as would exist if there were no tear. Use a pencil to draw a rectangle around the taped section, about 1 inch larger all around than the tape. Then, with sailcloth of the same weight and stretch characteristics as the torn sail, use shears to cut out a patch 1 inch larger all around than the penciled rectangle.

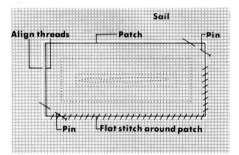

Make sure the lines of the threads in the patch and the sail go in the same direction (above). Seal the cut edges of the patch to prevent raveling, as explained at the far right. Turn the sail over and pin or tape the patch so it is centered over the penciled rectangle.

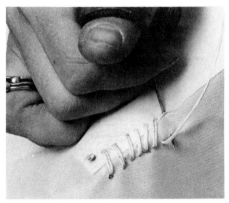

Sew the edges of the patch to the sail, using a flat stitch (above) that enters the sail 3/16 inch outside the edge of the patch and comes up through the patch 3/16 inch inside its edge. (With a flat stitch, the needle is thrust down and back through the cloth in one continuous motion so you do not have to turn the sail over every time you push the needle through.)

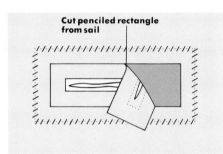

Turn the sail over again so the penciled rectangle is facing you, with the patch below it. Use shears to cut out the penciled rectangle from the sail (above), being careful not to cut into the patch behind it.

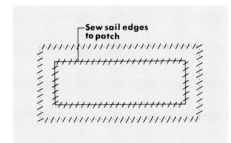

Seal the edges you have just cut. Then sew them to the patch (above), again using a flat stitch.

Sealing a cut edge

You must seal the edges of any sailcloth that you cut with shears, a process called hot knifing. By slightly melting the resn in the cloth, you can seal the cut threads to keep them from raveling.

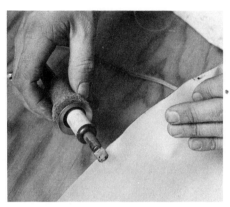

Use the tip of a soldering iron, rubbed along the raw edge of the cloth (above). Move steadily and gently along the edge. Don't stop in any one place or press hard. A properly sealed edge will show a uniform bead along its entire length, with no stray strands and no large blotches of resin.

Prolonging sail life

To prolong the life of your sail, rinse it with fresh water whenever salt or dirt accumulate on it. These abrade the weave and finish. Wash the sail occasionally in a bathtub, using lukewarm water and a mild detergent. Avoid hot water or abrasive cleansers. Dry the sail completely before you stow it away. Oil and grease can be removed with trichlorethylene, rust stains by soaking in a two-percent solution of hydrochloric acid and warm water. Whichever you use, complete the job by rinsing several times with fresh water (this is important). Fold the sail neatly for stowing, always making the folds parallel to the bottom. If you have space, roll up the sail, again parallel to the bottom, to avoid creases. Stow in a clean, dry, well-ventilated locker. Do not leave your sail out in the damaging ultraviolet rays of sunlight any longer than necessary. Repair worn stitching and minor tears before they become major ones.

1: Using chalk and a wood strip as a guide, draw the basic outlines of the sail on the floor.

2: The panels of sailcloth that make up the sail are rolled out so that they are at right angles to the diagonal line of the sail. Here the upper panels are in place and the bottom panel is being rolled toward what will become the bottom inside corner of the sail, as indicated in Figure E.

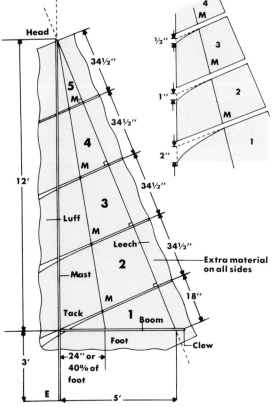

Figure E: A line drawn from the top of the sail to a point two-fifths of the distance between the inner and outer bottom corners intersects the edge of each panel at the point marked M. Detail (above, right) shows the tapers to be cut from the three lower panels to those points.

1844

Outdoor Activities
Marconi sail for a dinghy

A good project for a beginning sail maker is a simple triangular sail—one like the Marconi rig shown in Figure A (page 1840) and in the photograph on page 1839—which can be used to propel a small dinghy. The name dinghy is applied to a variety of small boats that are propelled by oars, sails, or small outboard motors. They are used in calm, sheltered waters for fishing or sailing, or as tenders for larger boats, enabling you to go back and forth between the large boat's mooring and the shore.

Dinghies come with flat, round, or V-shaped bottoms, and they vary in width, length, and weight. Generally a light, narrow boat is more easily driven through the water and so requires less sail power. A wide, heavy boat requires more power but can support larger sails. A flat-bottom dinghy tends to be more stable and can carry more sail than the equivalent boat with a round-bottom or V-bottom hull. To keep things on the safe side, the Marconi rig I have chosen for this project calls for 30 square feet of sail. This is midway between the 20-square-foot minimum and 40-square-foot maximum generally considered safe for an 8-foot-long dinghy. A non racing 14-foot dinghy should not carry more than 100 square feet of sail, and 45 square feet should give it adequate power. If you have a dinghy this large, the plans that follow can be scaled up to that size, but it is not advisable to go over 45 square feet unless you are an experienced sailor.

To make the sail for the 8-foot dinghy, you will need the following materials: 12 yards of 3.8-ounce soft-finish Dacron sailcloth (nominal width is 36 inches, actual width is 35 inches); 1 spool of V-69 polyester thread; 1 roll ¼-inch-wide clear adhesive tape that is sticky on both sides (Seamstik is one brand); three 1-inch-diameter No. 2 bronze grommets; six ½-inch-diameter No. 00 bronze grommets; several No. 15 sewing machine needles; 35 feet of 3.8-ounce Dacron tape 2 inches wide; and one ½-by-1-inch strip of wood 15 feet long that will bend to an even curve (ash is best), to serve as a guide when you draw the curves on the sail.

For tools, you will need: a sewing machine with zigzag attachment; a grommet hole cutter, grommet die and inserting punch for the No. 2 and No. 00 grommets; a soldering iron; eight awls (nails can be substituted if you can't borrow enough awls); a wooden mallet; large, sharp shears; white blackboard chalk; and a lead pencil.

The sailcloth, thread, tape, grommet hole cutter, die, punch, and grommets can be obtained at marine hardware stores or boatyards, or by mail from Alan-Clarke Sailmakers, Inc., 220 Route 25A, Northport, N. Y. 11768.

If you do not have a vertical mast and a horizontal boom for your dinghy (Figure E) ask the manufacturer of your dinghy where you can get them. If it was not originally designed with a sail plan, consult the sources listed above or check the equipment directories published by yachting periodicals. Spruce is the most popular wood for these two spars; it is sometimes laminated for additional strength. Aluminum is stronger, stiffer, and will probably cost more.

As a work area, you will need a wooden floor at least 5 feet wider and longer than the maximum dimensions of your sail. The best bets are a basement shop with a wooden floor or an unused attic. The chalk marks you make will wash off easily, but the holes you make with awls or nails may be more of a problem.

Laying Out the Sail

First, measure the length of your mast and boom (Figure E). Ours measured 15 feet and 5½ feet respectively. By allowing 3 feet at the bottom of the mast, to leave enough room for people to sit comfortably in the boat under the sail, and 6 inches at the end of the horizontal boom, I arrived at a vertical sail dimension (the luff) of 12 feet and a horizontal sail dimension (the foot) of 5 feet (Figure E). A line drawn from the top point of the sail (the head) to the outside bottom corner (the clew) establishes the triangle within which the sail will be set. Wet the blackboard chalk and, using the long strip of wood as a guide, draw this triangle on the floor (photograph 1). Extend the lines about a foot past their three points of intersection so you will have visible guidelines after you lay the cloth on the floor. Now take the sailcloth and roll out panels at right angles to the diagonal chalk line that will be the diagonal edge (the leech) of the sail (photograph 2). Cut each panel, allowing 4 inches of extra cloth extending beyond each side of your outline on the floor. Arrange the sail panels so that the top edge of the bottom panel runs directly into the inside bottom corner (the tack), as in Figure E and photograph 2. This is called the home seam. Note that it is necessary to trim a considerable amount of sailcloth off the bottom panel to make it conform to the outline needed.

With a pencil, draw a line on the sailcloth from the top of the sail to a point two-fifths of the distance between the inside bottom corner and the outside bottom corner (Figure E). On our sail, two-fifths of 5 feet comes to 2 feet. This penciled line, extending from the bottom to the top of the sail, marks the location of the deepest part of the curve you will build into the sail. It is called the maximum draft point and will intersect each panel 40 percent of the sail behind the mast.

Along the vertical edge of the sail, mark off tapers 2 inches wide, 1 inch wide, and ½ inch wide on the top edge of the panels marked 1, 2, and 3 in Figure E. For the bottom seam, mark the taper on an extension of the vertical edge, 2 inches below the line that will eventually be the bottom edge of the sail. With the long, flexible wooden strip as a guide, mark a curve from point M (Figure E) on each of the three panels, to the taper mark on the vertical edge of the sail (photograph 3). With a pencil draw in this curve on the sailcloth. Cut along the line. You should be cutting off a tapering sliver that gradually decreases in size as your shears move from the vertical edge of the sail in towards point M (photograph 4). Seal the cut edges of sailcloth with a soldering iron (Craftnotes, page 1843).

Apply double-stick tape along the bottom edge of panels 2, 3, 4, and 5, between the outer edge of the panel and the selvage line. Beginning in the middle of each panel at point M and moving outward, first toward the inside edge of the sail and then toward the diagonal outside edge, stick the upper edge of each panel to the bottom of the panel above it (photograph 5). Here you must be very careful to maintain equal tension from one edge of the sail to the other on each pair of panels; one must not be tighter than the other. Equally important, you must overlap the top edge of each panel exactly to the ½-inch selvage line of the panel above it. If you fail to match these lines, you will not have good tapers, and you will create an uneven shape in your sail.

3: To mark the small triangular tapers to be cut in the forward portion of the sail panels (Figure E), use your knee to hold the wood strip at the maximum taper point. Bend the strip until it touches point M and draw the taper curve.

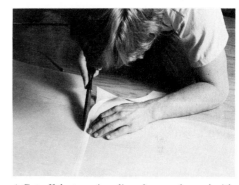

4: Cut off the tapering sliver from each panel with large shears, moving from the vertical edge of the sail in toward point M (Figure E).

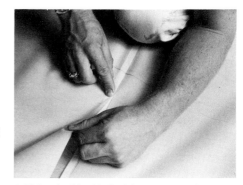

5: Using double-sided sticky tape, stick the upper edge of each panel to the ½-inch selvage on the bottom of the panel above it. Keep equal tension on both panels as you work from the midpoint out to each edge.

6: When sewing the sail panels together, keep the two rows of zigzag stitches inside each edge of the seam and about ⅛ inch apart.

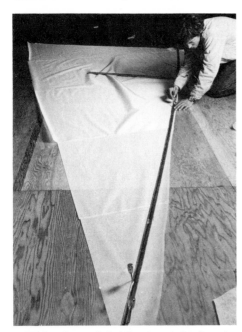

7: With awls or nails holding the wood strip at the top and the bottom inside corners of the sail, bend the strip so that it bulges 2 inches beyond the vertical line of the sail, at a point one-third of the way up from the bottom inside corner (Figure F). Fix the bent strip in this position with awls or nails; then use it as a guide for drawing the curved line on the panels from the top to the bottom of the sail.

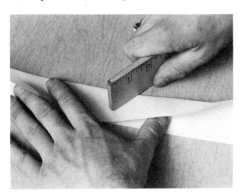

8: Fold the Dacron tape that becomes the edging on the sail in half along its entire length and crease with a ruler. Then slip it over the edge of the sail, and sew in place with a zigzag stitch.

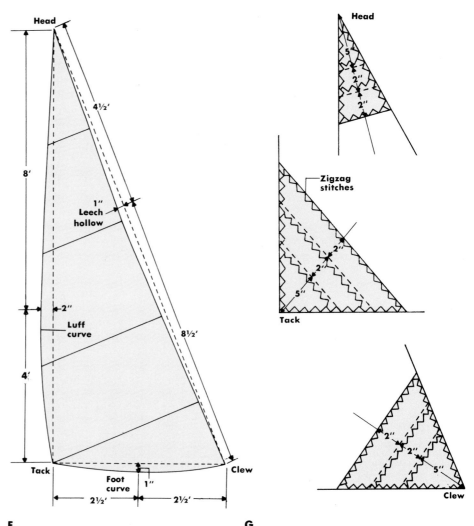

F

Figure F: Here are the depths and locations of the three curves you need to cut on the three edges of the triangular sail. A leech hollow on the outer edge is needed on small sails that do not have wood stiffening strips inserted in them.

G

Figure G: Cut three patches for each corner of the sail. Attach the patches to the sail in the order described in the text, using sticky tape. Then sew them to the sail, with a zigzag stitch around the edges and where the patches overlap.

Sew the panels together with a double row of zigzag stitching (photograph 6). Keep the two rows of stitching straight and ⅛ inch apart, just inside each seam edge.

With the sewing finished, return to the floor. Lay the sail out flat. With the long, flexible wooden strip, lay out a straight line from the top of the sail to the inside bottom corner. Fix the wooden strip at both points with awls or nails, placing one on each side. Then push the strip gently outward along the lower part of the line extending from the top to the inside bottom corner of the sail, as in photograph 7. The strip should make a smooth, convex curve with its deepest point about 2 inches outside the straight line between the top of the sail and the bottom inside corner. This point should be about one-third of the way up from the bottom inside corner (Figure F). Hold the curve in the wood strip with several awls or nails placed snugly on each side of the strip along its entire length. With the strip as a guide, use a pencil to mark the curve on the cloth.

Perform the same operation between the inside bottom corner and the outside bottom corner of the sail. Your bulge here should also be convex and a maximum of 1 inch deep, with that point halfway between the corners (Figure F). Between the top and the outside bottom corner of the sail, you can mark the diagonal edge, a concave curve called a leech hollow. This is advisable for sails that do not have battens (stiffening strips of wood) inserted in them. Fix the wood strip to produce an indentation that is 1 inch deep at a point 8½ feet up from the outside bottom corner (Figure F). Use the wood strip as a guide to draw the line for this curve. Cut out the sail along the lines you have laid down for all three curved edges, using shears.

From your roll of sailcloth, cut three triangular patches for each corner of the sail, nine patches in all (Figure G). Seal the cut edges with a soldering iron (Craftnotes, page 1843). The patches should conform to the outline of the sail at each corner and should be 5, 7, and 9 inches in height. It makes no difference on which side of the sail you place the patches, as long as they are all on one side. The largest patch should be on the outside, with the medium-sized patch against the sail and the smallest patch in the middle. Starting with the medium-sized patch, fix all three patches in place on each corner of the sail, using double-stick tape. Make sure you maintain even tension between patch and sail. Sew on the patches with a zigzag stitch (Figure G). Sew along each edge as close as you can get without straying off the patch.

Measure and cut lengths of 2-inch-wide Dacron tape (the same weight as the sailcloth, 3.8-ounce in this case) to cover each of the three curved edges of the sail. Fold the tape in half down its entire length, and crease the fold by rubbing it with the edge of a ruler (photograph 8). Slip the tape over the edge of the sailcloth, and sew each length to its respective edge, maintaining equal tension between the sailcloth and the tape. Use a zigzag stitch and stay as close to the edge of the tape as you can without wandering off onto the sailcloth. The tapes should overlap at the corners.

Put 1-inch-diameter grommets into the three corners of the sail and half-a-dozen ½-inch-diameter grommets at 22-inch intervals up the vertical edge of the sail, starting at the bottom inside corner (Figure H and Craftnotes, page 1842). The large grommets at the inside and outside bottom corners should be centered about 1¼ inches in from each corner on a line that bisects the angle formed by the edges of the sail. At the top corner of the sail, the grommet should be about 1½ inches in, enough to make sure that the grommet is fully on the sail. For the smaller grommets, place the center ¾ inch in from the vertical edge of the sail. After the grommets have been set in place, trim off the sharp points at all three corners with shears (photograph 9). You are now ready to fix your sail in place and go sailing.

For related projects, see "Canoeing," "Hammocks and Slings," "Kayaks," "Piloting Small Boats," "Ship Models," "Weather Forecasting."

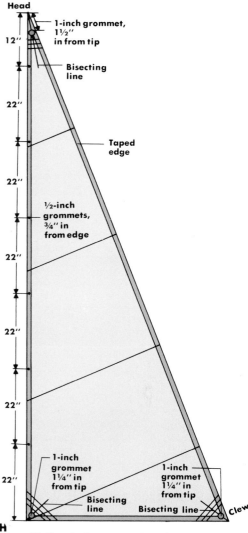

Figure H: Set 1-inch grommets in each corner and ½ inch grommets along the vertical edge of the sail as shown, following the techniques given in the Craftnotes, page 1842.

9: After the grommets have been mounted in each corner, cut off sharp corner points with shears.

Making a jib

While an 8-foot dinghy is too small for a jib sail, in light winds a jib can be used effectively and safely on 10- to 14-foot dinghies. The size of such a jib sail should not be more than 20 square feet for a 10-foot dinghy, or 40 square feet for a 14-footer.

Making a jib sail follows the same principles and techniques explained in the text for making a Marconi mainsail, except that the diagonal curve, here the leading edge of the sail, must take into account a slight sag in the line that holds it. No matter how tightly that line is tied, it will not be able to hold the leading edge of the sail as straight as the mast holds the mainsail. With the pressure of the wind and the weight of the sail, the edge will sag (as from dotted straight line above, right). To compensate for this, the curve to be cut must be less round toward the bottom where it is deepest on a mainsail, and must actually be concave toward the top where the mainsail curve flattens out. The result is that a shallow S-shaped curve needs to be cut on the leading edge of a jib sail (below, right).

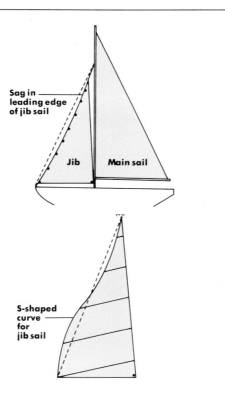

Sag in leading edge of jib sail

Jib   Main sail

S-shaped curve for jib sail

The young girl in the silhouette on the wall, Becca Read of Putney, Vermont, stitched the sampler (dated June 19, 1800) on the table. The sewing basket, needlecase, scissors, and brass eyeglasses belonged to Sally Steele George of New Sharon, Maine. The tin spool holder, clamp-on iron pincushion, embroidery hoop, and Shaker darning egg date from the nineteenth century. Everything shown is from the collection of Glee Krueger of Westport, Connecticut.

SAMPLERS
Xs Make the Message

Bernice Barsky of New York designs handcraft projects for magazines and yarn companies. On one assignment, she adapted pre-Columbian textile designs to make needlepoint kits for the Metropolitan Museum of Art. She enjoys translating needlecraft directions written in French and Italian, owned a yarn shop for ten years, and has been a mechanical draftsman and technical editor. Bernice studied at the Pratt-New York Phoenix School of Design, The Fashion Institute of Technology and Mechanics Institute in New York, and the Philadelphia College of Textiles and Science.

The kind of needlework samplers that are being worked today—with pictorial scenes, alphabets, numerals, verses, and borders of flowers done mostly in cross-stitch on even-weave fabric—evolved largely in America and England during the period between 1750 and 1840.

Before then, as far back as Elizabethan times, a sampler was a collection of many different embroidery stitches worked on a long, narrow strip of handwoven linen. Stitches, especially those that were new or particularly difficult, could be referred to as necessary. Samplers of lace patterns and knitting stitches were made for the same reason, also being worked in long strips.

Many samplers of the late eighteenth and early nineteenth centuries were done by children remarkably young, during their school years and even before. This was a time when a young girl's education consisted mainly of mastering needlework, etiquette, and religious beliefs. Samplers were exercises in embroidery skills, of course, but they also tested to some extent a child's neatness, spelling, and knowledge of the Bible. In samplers made by older girls in certain finishing schools, the influence of a few teachers can be found in the similarity of the designs and verses. Some of the more elaborate samplers took months and even years to complete.

The earliest American sampler still in existence, now displayed in Pilgrim Hall at Plymouth, Massachusetts, was made around 1640 by Loara Standish, daughter of Captain Miles Standish.

A detail of the bottom section of a sampler made by Lois Tillson in 1760 is one of the earliest samplers to show an umbrella or parasol (held by the middle figure in the pink dress). Stitches include: two-color rice, cross, satin, oriental, outline, and eyelet. The sampler is American and possibly was done in Massachusetts.

Below: This small ruffled sampler was made in England by Ann Ward in the nineteenth century. The stylized floral and animal motifs and the central verse are done in red cross-stitches on a bleached linen ground. The sampler is 6 inches high by 6⅜ inches wide, with a ¾-inch ruffle added.

An English sampler fragment depicting the Garden of Eden, 9 inches high by 8¾ inches wide, is stitched with silk threads on a linen background. The fig leaves on the figures of Adam and Eve are worked in a detached buttonhole stitch and attached separately. The sampler dates from 1727.

Antique Samplers

The antique samplers and fragments of samplers on these pages are from the collection of Glee Krueger of Westport, Connecticut. Mrs. Krueger was on the staff of the Art Institute of Chicago and is the author of a book on New England samplers. The samplers shown here date from the seventeenth, eighteenth, and nineteenth centuries and were worked in America, England, and Canada.

An example of embroidery done on perforated or punched paper is this ribbon-backed bookmark worked in wool, silk twist, and steel beads. The inscription reads: "Presented to Mrs. Ruth Goodale by Mager John Button living in Canada aged 81 years Sept. 1853/Remember me." The bookmark is 2⅝ inches high by 8¼ inches wide.

Young boys stitched samplers too—George Parker, born May 30, 1791, made this sampler in 1799 in Bradford, Massachusetts. He worked with silk floss and twist threads on linen; the sampler is 12½ inches high by 11 inches wide.

An embroidered pincushion 2⅛ inches square commemorating the marriage of Queen Victoria to Prince Albert, February 10, 1840, was stitched by a child in England's Cheltenham Female Orphan Asylum. One side proclaims that "A virtuous woman is a (crown) to her husband." The silk cross-stitches are on a gauze ground, with silk tassels at the corners.

This sampler fragment from England has the maker's name, Rachel Cormel, and the year, 1678, done in eyelet stitch; the alphabet is done in satin stitch. Portions of the design are appliqued, as a comparison of the front side (left) and the back side (right) shows. The original vivid colors used for the deep border at the bottom are apparent on the back; they appear quite muted on the front. The sampler is silk on linen, 13¾ inches high by 7½ inches wide.

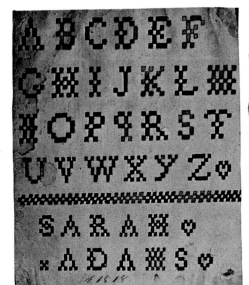

This draft, or pattern, for a sampler alphabet is in two tones of brown ink on paper. It was made by Sarah Adams, an American, in 1818, and was found in New York. It is 7½ inches high by 6¼ inches wide.

Right: Hannah Loring of Lebanon, Connecticut, wrought this charming pictorial sampler with several alphabets and a verse in October, 1834; she was taught needlework by Ann Beaumont. The sampler is silk on linen canvas, 17¼ inches high by 18½ inches wide.

This sampler, made by Harriet Peverly of Canterbury, New Hampshire in 1826, is elaborately bordered on three sides. Stitches include: rococco, cross, stem, bullion, satin, hem, herringbone, oriental, straight, long-armed cross, slanting Gobelin, and French knot. It was worked in silk on a linen ground and is 16⅝ inches high by 16½ inches wide.

Elizabeth Smith, aged 10, chose a dark green linsey-woolsey fabric (linen warp, wool filling) for the background of her sampler, made in America in 1816. The embroidery is silk; the stitches include: satin, cross, eyelet and oriental. The sampler is 15¾ inches high by 16¾ inches wide.

Needlecrafts
A pegboard sampler

Cross-stitching a name in big block letters across a pegboard is a good way for a young child to practice embroidery. On graph paper, plot the child's name in Xs to determine how much pegboard you will need. Pegboard holes are spaced 1 inch apart, and one cross-stitch will use four holes—two across and two down. A short name, such as Jackie, will fit on a board 12 by 36 inches, as pictured below, left. A longer name will need a longer board; a two-part name can be stitched in two rows on a wider board.

Have the pegboard cut to size; then spray one side with two coats of white enamel. Heavyweight rug yarn (one skein) and a blunt tapestry or rug needle with a large eye make the stitching go quickly and easily.

Stitching on pegboard is good practice for the proper two-handed method of embroidering. One hand is held on top of the work and the other hand below; the needle is passed through the work from one hand to the other (photograph 1). When fabric is used, this results in smoother stitches and causes less distortion of the weave than inserting the needle in and out of two points in a single motion.

Making knots at the ends of threads is not a good idea on fabric because the knots show through and cause bumps, but there is no problem when the fabric is a stiff sheet of pegboard (photograph 2). Ends too short to be knotted can be taped down.

When the cross-stitches are done, hang the pegboard and insert hooks to hold his or her paraphernalia.

Jackie now has a special place to hang her hats, and she can proudly say it is a sample of her embroidery talents. The pegboard was sprayed with white enamel; the cross-stitches are made with brightly colored rug yarn.

1: Jackie works intently on her pegboard sampler, using two hands to pass the needle back and forth, while Trin looks on.

2: Knots can be used to end a length of yarn on the back of the pegboard because they do not show or cause bumps. Short ends can be taped flat.

Needlecrafts
Hoop-framed samplers

¢ ⊠ 👫 🦎

Using gingham or dotted swiss as a background fabric lets a beginner count checks or dots instead of counting threads when she makes a sampler. And embroidery hoops made of colorful plastic or natural wood can be used as frames when the embroidery is done. For these reasons, hoop-framed sampler pictures done on either fabric are ideal projects for children.

A round hoop 8 inches in diameter, preferably with a screw-type adjustment, is a good size for small, inexperienced hands. A hoop works well for embroidery of this size because the fabric does not need to be moved. For larger samplers, a frame is preferable; moving a hoop from one area to another could damage stitches caught under the top hoop. Choose either a tapestry (blunt) or a chenille (pointed) needle, and use six-strand embroidery floss, pearl cotton, or light-to-medium weight yarn.

Cut a 12-inch square of gingham (⅛-, ¼-, or ½-inch checks) and a square of the same size from a man's white handkerchief to use as the lining. Put the two layers of fabric between the hoops and pull them taut (photograph 3, page 1856).

Following one of the cross-stitch charts on page 1856, or any chart for a simple design that can be contained within the hoop area, locate the center of the chart and the center of fabric. Then decide where to start the first stitch (photograph 4, page 1857). If the design is at all complicated, it is best to start in the center and work out toward the edges. On simple designs such as those shown here, you can work from

Jennifer used dotted swiss instead of gingham so she could follow the dots as she worked the stitches of her flower with variegated floss.

Trin didn't stop with a purple chick; she added a stretch of grass and a flower to her gingham-background sampler picture.

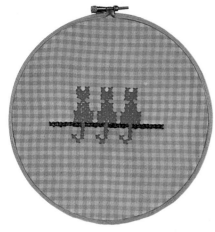

Grace embroidered a trio of cats on ⅛-inch gingham checks. She gave the design a personal touch by providing them with a fence to sit on.

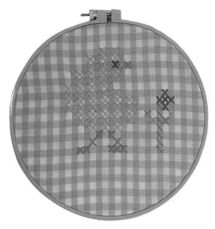

Joanna followed a chart to make her cheery yellow chick, then added her own flower design. The basic charts are given in Figure A, page 1856.

CRAFTNOTES: STITCHES

Cross-stitch
Make a row of evenly spaced, slanting stitches, starting at the lower right corner and working from right to left. Work back, completing the Xs. Be sure that all top stitches cross in the same direction and that all stitches meet at the corners. (Cross-stitches may be worked from left to right, if that is more comfortable for you.)

French knot
Wrap the thread several times around the needle, holding the thread taut. Insert the needle close to the starting point; pull it through slowly and keep the knot close to the surface.

Straight stitch
Bring the needle through at one end, and insert it at the other end, making a single stitch. Carry the needle under the fabric to the start of the next stitch, leaving space between the stitches.

Stem stitch
Working from left to right, take regular, slightly slanting stitches along the line of the design. Bring the thread through on the left side of the previous stitch, and keep it below the needle.

Filled-in running stitch
Run the needle over and under the fabric, making the upper stitches equal or unequal lengths as needed. Work back, filling in the spaces.

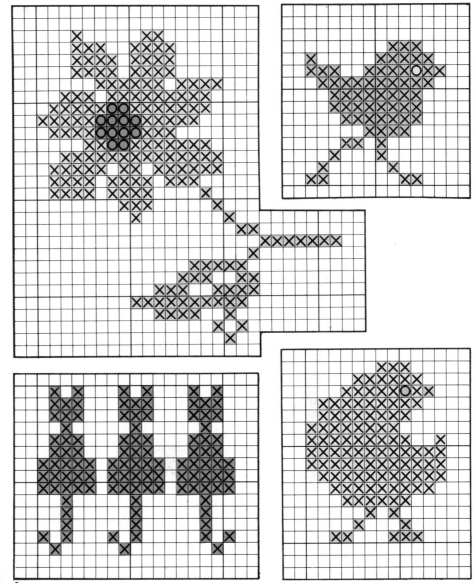

A
Figure A: The embroidery charts above are for the flower, the two chicks, and the trio of cats that appear on the hoop-framed samplers, page 1855. Cats and chicks are stitched on the denim patches, page 1858, and a lone cat is stitched on the sampler on page 1859.

3: Joanna makes sure that both layers of fabric, the gingham and the lining, are unwrinkled and taut in the hoops.

the top down or, for that matter, in any direction. If you find the fabric needs to be moved on the hoops in order to center the design, do so as soon as the basic motif or a key part of it is completed (photograph 5).

Add extra designs to fill in the background if you like, when you are sure the main design is centered. If the fabric stays in the hoops in a wrong position for any length of time, you may need to iron it before repositioning it. Iron the cross-stitches on the wrong side, face down on a terry cloth towel, to avoid flattening them.

To thread thick yarn through the needle, pinch the yarn around the needle below the eye (photograph 6) and push the eye onto this doubled end (photograph 7). To secure an end of yarn, pull it through a few stitches on the back; do not make knots. If the end is very short, unthread the needle and push it through a few stitches until the eye aligns with the end of the yarn. Then thread the yarn through the eye and pull the needle through (photograph 8).

When the embroidery is finished, round the corners of the excess fabric and gather up the edges (both layers together) with basting stitches, pulling the excess inside the hoop on the back. Secure the gathering stitches. Hang the hoop on a hook, using a length of matching yarn or ribbon.

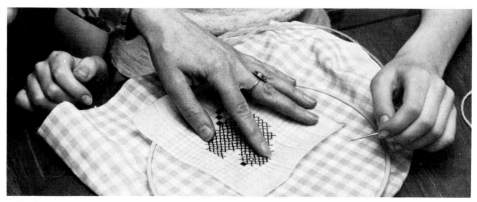

4: Craftswoman Bernice Barsky shows Joanna how to center her design on the fabric. With the first stitch in place as the starting point, Joanna will simply count the Xs in each row of the chart and fill in a corresponding number of squares on the gingham.

5: Grace shows her first cross-stitch cat. If she finds that the design is off-center, she can unscrew the top hoop and move the fabric.

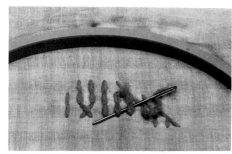

6: To thread sport-weight yarn through the eye of the tapestry needle, first pinch it tightly around the needle, leaving an end an inch or so long.

7: Then slide the yarn off the needle without losing the crease; push the eye of the needle onto this loop and pull the loop through.

8: To secure a short end, work the unthreaded needle under a few stitches until you align the eye with the yarn end, thread it and pull it through.

Joanna concentrates as she checks the chart for the number of stitches she still must make in the body of the chick.

Trin holds her hoop with one hand and passes the needle from the back to the front through the same hole as the neighboring stitch.

Next, she passes the needle in the opposite direction. This two-step method results in uniform stitches and does not pull the fabric.

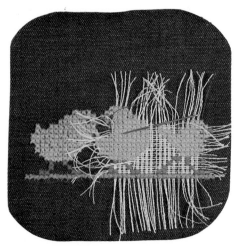

9: Baste cross-stitch canvas onto the denim patch, embroider through the patch and over the canvas meshes (as you would over threads of even-weave fabric), then gently pull out the canvas threads with your fingers or tweezers.

An iron-on denim patch, embroidered with a pair of fat cats, can be used to decorate a book bag or a pair of jeans. Variegated embroidery floss can give the cats a sun-dappled look.

Needlecrafts
A patch of denim

Counting threads on an iron-on denim patch would be virtually impossible—but it is possible to embroider such a patch with cross-stitches, and to keep those stitches as straight and even as though you could count the threads. The secret is cross-stitch canvas. It looks like a thin penelope needlepoint canvas, with a dark vertical thread every five meshes to help you keep count. You simply baste this cross-stitch canvas on top of the denim patch (or any other uneven-weave or hard-to-count fabric); then work your stitches through both layers. Count the threads of the canvas as you would count the threads of an even-weave fabric, and make the cross-stitches over the meshes, keeping them even but not too tight. When the embroidery is finished, cut off the excess canvas and gently pull out the threads from underneath the cross-stitches (photograph 9). To avoid crushing the stitches, use a terry cloth towel as a press cloth when you iron the patch onto a tote bag or jeans.

Needlecrafts
Design your own sampler

Many things can be translated into charts for samplers—drawings from a child's coloring book, photographs from a magazine, a fabric print, needlepoint charts, greeting card designs. The personalized sampler shown on the opposite page is an invitation for a boy named Richard to visit his grandparents; the elements could be modified to make such a sampler appeal to any child. In this case, the fabric was pulled taut and thumb-tacked to the back of a canvas-stretcher frame from an art store; this kept it smooth while it was being worked. The finished sampler can be displayed in a picture frame under glass if that is desirable.

To create your own design, use graph paper to trace the design—the transparent kind used by draftsmen is ideal. Or you can hold ordinary graph paper up to a window and trace the design behind it. Still another alternative that works well with simple, large designs is to make your own graph on tracing paper; then outline the shape and fill in with Xs. Square off any rounded edges to fit into the squares of the graph paper and simplify complicated designs. Trace on the wrong side of the graph paper so that if you must erase, you will not erase the graph lines. You can vary the size of the design by changing the size of the graph paper (how many squares it has per inch) or by plotting each stitch over more than one square. For example, wide cross-stitches can be made one square high and three squares wide; tall stitches can be one square wide and two squares high.

When planning a sampler with several motifs, use thread to baste the outlines of the major elements on the fabric. This helps you visualize how the finished sampler will look, and you can rearrange motifs before they are stitched. Remove the basting threads after the embroidery is completed.

The background fabric can be any cloth with an even weave, such as linen, hardanger cloth, loose-weave wool, panama cloth, *aida* cloth, or *herta* cloth. The thread can be one or more strands of pearl cotton, six-strand embroidery cotton, crewel wool, tapestry yarn, or silk or metallic threads. Check your local art needlework shop, or order from the mail-order sources listed on page 1860.

The sampler shown on page 1859 has an actual design area 12 by 16½ inches. It is worked primarily in crewel wools and the background fabric is hardanger cloth. Charts for the alphabet and major design elements are given in Figures B and C, pages 1859 and 1860. The basic stitch is cross-stitch; the dark blue tree tops are straight stitch; the border has an inner row of stem stitch and two outer rows of cross-stitch. The roof of the house is half-cross-stitch (four threads high by two threads wide); the doors and windows are small cross-stitches (two threads square) surrounding large cross-stitches (four threads square). The alphabet, small sailboat, birds, and animals are worked in small cross-stitches (two threads square); the house, cars, truck, train, large boats, airplanes, and green trees are large cross-stitches (four threads square).

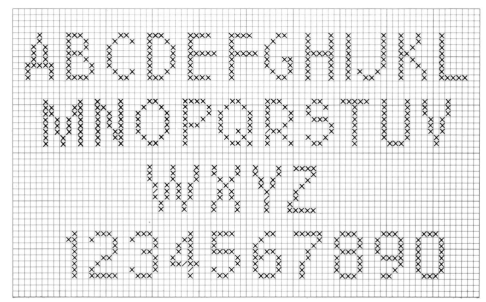

Richard will remember this invitation to visit his grandparents for years to come, since it will hang in his room. Many different elements of interest to him make this sampler very personally his.

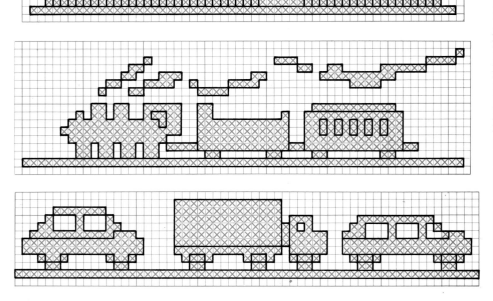

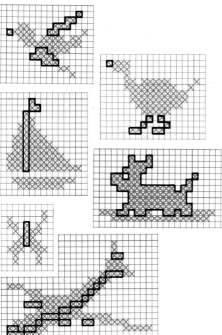

B
Figure B: Charts for the alphabet and nine elements of the sampler, shown above right, are given. Although the sailboat appears in two sizes on the sampler, the same chart is used. In the small boat, each cross-stitch is worked over a two-by-two-thread square on the fabric; in the large boat, each stitch is worked over a four-by-four-thread square. This technique can be used with any chart to reduce or enlarge the size of the motif. Charts for six other elements used on the sampler are given in Figure C, page 1860.

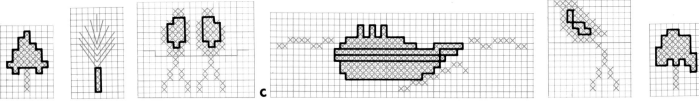

Figure C: Charts for additional elements used in the sampler on page 1859 are given above.

Needlecrafts
Perforated-paper sampler ¢ ● ♟ ⏰

Janet Fiori of Sea Cliff, New York, is a free-lance designer who specializes in doing embroidery on perforated paper, although she does many other types of stitchery as well. Her designs have been published and she teaches this Victorian craft to women's groups and children in her neighborhood.

Samplers, bookmarks, and greeting cards embroidered on perforated paper instead of cloth were popular during the nineteenth century, but their popularity so waned that by the late 1940s this special-purpose paper was no longer made. An example of an old perforated-paper bookmark is shown on page 1850.

The paper is again available and this almost-forgotten needlecraft is being revived. You can order sheets of the perforated paper from Sewmakers Incorporated, 1619 Grand Avenue, Baldwin, New York 11510. The traditional way to embroider on the special paper is to stitch in the design only, leaving the cream-colored background unworked.

The sampler pictured at left is embroidered with three strands of six-strand embroidery cotton in five colors: light, medium, and dark green; medium and dark coral. The filled-in running stitch alphabets (top) are dark green; the cross-stitch alphabets (bottom) are medium green; the single motifs between the alphabets combine light green and light coral; all other stitches are either medium green or dark coral. Charts for the alphabets, borders, and single motifs are given in Figure D; refer to the color photograph, left, for their placement.

Stitching on perforated paper is much like stitching on fabric, with a few exceptions (photographs 10 and 11). Because the paper is stiff, you cannot crush the sides to reach the center or put the paper in a hoop, although you can tack it to a frame. The paper does not ravel, so finishing the edges is unnecessary. Select a blunt, slender needle with a long eye. Use two separate motions to make a stitch—do not work the needle in and out of two holes in a single motion. Work evenly and do not pull the stitches very tight. Use thread no thicker than three strands of embroidery cotton to avoid tearing the holes, and stitch over loose ends in back to hold them rather than make knots. When crossing from one letter to the next on the back, use a diagonal stitch to minimize show-through.

For related entries, see "Crewel," "Embroidery," "Hardanger," "Needlepoint."

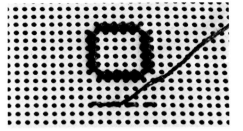

10: The design elements are done in cross-stitch (top) and filled-in running stitch (bottom). The back side of the paper is less smooth and shiny than the front side.

11: Cross from one letter to another on the back side with a diagonal, rather than a horizontal, stitch to minimize show-through. Indicate the center of the sheet with pencil lines on the back.

This alphabet-and-borders sampler is stitched in soft shades of green and coral on perforated paper. As shown, the overall size is 11 by 14 inches (157 by 201 holes), but you can combine the various elements in Figure D to make a larger or smaller sampler. The top alphabets are worked in filled-in running stitch; the bottom alphabets are done in cross-stitch (see Craftnotes, page 1855).

D Figure D: Charts for the alphabets, border designs, and single motifs for the paper sampler are given above; combine them any way you like or follow the color photograph opposite for placement. The filled-in running stitches for the top alphabets cross over one or more holes to give letters the proper slant and height.

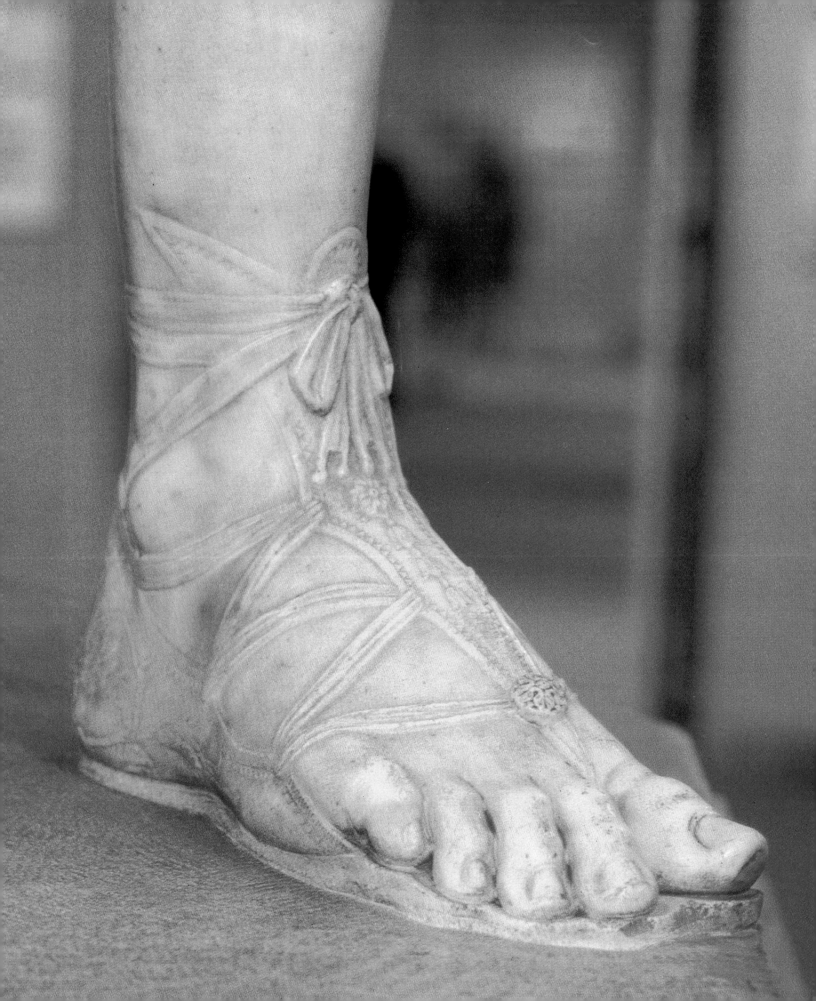

5: Wearing rubber gloves to protect your hands, use a cotton rag to wipe leather dye onto the leather that will be used for the straps, matching the color of the top layer of the sole.

6: Use a metal ruler or straightedge to guide the hooked leather knife as you cut the four ½-inch-wide straps, each 36 inches long, that you need for the two sandals.

7: With a water-based dye prepared for this purpose, stain the long edges of the four straps. Be careful not to get any stain on the top surface of the strap.

8: Insert two of the straps in the front slots so that ½ inch of each protrudes on the bottom side of the sole. Cross the straps on the top side to establish the desired angle.

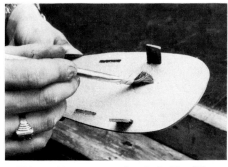

9: Using rubber cement, glue the inside of the protruding strap end to the bottom of the sole. Put rubber cement on both surfaces; then set the sandal aside until the cement is tacky.

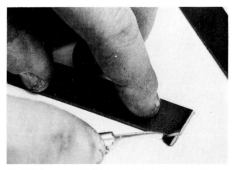

10: While you wait (at least 15 minutes), cut two upright ankle straps, each ½ by 3¼ inches. At one end, angle the corners and make two ½-inch slots. Then dye the edges.

11: By now the rubber cement on the sole and toe straps should be ready to be joined. Press the ends of the straps firmly against the bottom of the sole for a few moments.

12: Insert the upright ankle straps in the slots near the heel, with the trimmed ends pointing up. Glue the bottom ends as you did with the toe straps.

13: To thread the long straps through the sandal, cross the straps over each other and insert the free ends into the wider center slots (cut wider so two strips can pass through, side by side).

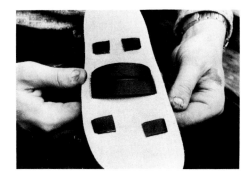

14: Make sure the straps parallel each other across the bottom, and thread each back through the opposite center slot. Crossed straps here would cause an uncomfortable bump.

15: Cross the two long straps again over the instep, and thread them through the parallel slots that you cut near the top of the upright ankle straps.

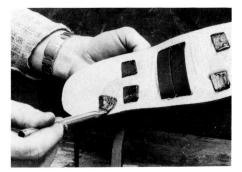

16: Put rubber cement on the bottom of the entire sole except for the parallel straps; these you want to leave free so they can be adjusted. Again, wait for the glue to get tacky.

17: Place the sandal on the thicker cowhide sole and press the inner sole down firmly. Then hammer the two layers together, using a flat-faced leather hammer that does not leave marks.

18: Using the hooked knife, cut away the cowhide to match the outline of the inner sole. The heavy cowhide may require four or five strokes of the knife before it is cut through.

19: With medium-grit sandpaper, smooth all around the two-layer edge of the sandal's sole. You can use a powered rotary sander if you have one.

20: With a tool called a beveler, round the edge of the sandal's sole on both top and bottom, giving it a neat, even finish. The beveler's two-pronged blade will cut off a thin sliver of leather.

21: To make an arch in the sandal's sole, you can wet the leather and bend it up on the inner side into the shape pictured. When the leather dries, it will hold the comfortable raised shape.

22: To make sure the layers of the sole hold together, hammer in brass brads ½ inch apart all around the edge. Drive them from the top. (If you want the sandal stitched, take it to a shoemaker.)

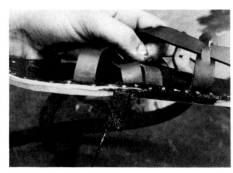

23: Using the water-based dye again, stain the entire edge of the sandal, including the bevels, but be careful not to get any of the stain on the top of the sole.

24: To make sure the ends of the straps and the uprights will not pull loose, hammer a brad into each strap, driving the brads from the top so they go through the hidden ½-inch ends of the straps.

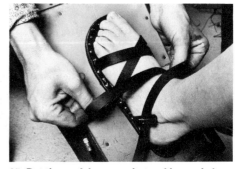

25: Put the sandal on your foot and have a helper adjust the front crossed straps by pulling on them where they emerge from the side slots in the middle of the sole.

26: With the straps at a comfortable tightness, bring the inside strap around the back of the heel, and mark the strap at the point where it crosses the ankle.

27: Bring the front strap around into position and mark it in the same place, using the back strap as a guide. Be sure the tension over the instep is comfortable.

28: Make a ½-inch slot on the inside strap with the mallet and slot-making tool, bridging the ankle mark. The buckle will be attached here; holes will be punched in the outside strap.

29: Slip the buckle through the slot, fold over the end, and with a rotary hole punch make a hole for a rivet through both layers of leather. Cut off the excess leather on this strap.

30: Place the strap on a wood block with the buckle in place. Put a brass rivet through the hole that was made with the hole punch, and hammer the rivet cap on the rivet.

31: With the rotary hole punch, make a hole on the ankle mark of the outside strap, then to make the strap adjustable, make several holes on either side of it. Trim off the excess strap.

Leathercrafts
The Italia

$ ▨ ⚊ ⚗

The Seville leather sandal (page 1864) can be easily modified by changing the placement of the straps. The Italia, pictured at right, has one strap across the toes and adjustable crossed straps over the instep that are threaded through ankle uprights and buckle on the outside. To make the sandal, follow the directions on pages 1864 through 1867, making the slots for the straps in the same places as shown in Figure A. But make the center slots only ½ inch long. Thread the ½-inch-wide, 36-inch-long strap through the toe slots, centering the strap between the two slots (Figure B). Cross the straps under the sole, bring them out at the middle slots, and cross them over the instep. Insert the ankle uprights in the heel slots and glue them in place. Thread the ends of the long straps through the slots in the uprights and finish the sandal, following the directions given for the Seville (opposite

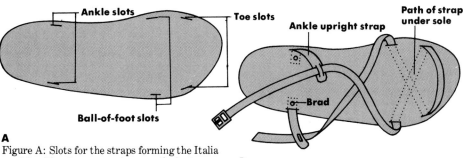

A
Figure A: Slots for the straps forming the Italia sandal, with only one crossing over the instep, are placed beside the toes, the ball of the foot, and the ankles. Position the slots while the foot pattern is being traced.

B
Figure B: Italia straps are threaded through the slots as shown. The dotted lines indicate how the strap crosses underneath the sole of the sandal.

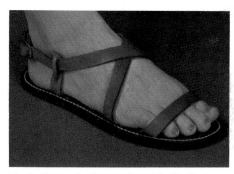

The Italia is a simpler version of the Seville leather sandal, with one strap that passes over the toes, crosses over the instep, is threaded through ankle upright straps, and closes with a buckle.

and above). To get the correct fit, put the sandal on your foot and mark the location of the buckle at your ankle. Attach the buckle, trim off excess leather, and punch holes as needed on the opposite strap.

Leathercrafts
The Riviera

$ ▨ ⚊ ⚗

Another variation of the Seville leather sandal, the Riviera, is a favorite among those who like a toe strap. The adjustable strap crossed over the instep is the same in the Riviera and the Italia. Follow the directions on pages 1864 through 1867, but make the strap slots as shown in Figure C (page 1868). The two toe slots are placed on either side of the big toe. The inside slot is placed at the base of the big toe, and the outside slot is placed at the ball of the foot. Heel slots, as in the other

Leather suppliers
Berman Leather Company
147 South Street
Boston, Mass. 02111

Indiana Leather and Supply Company
216 South Indiana Avenue
Bloomington, Ind. 47401

Tandy Leather
508 Avenue of the Americas
New York, N.Y. 10011

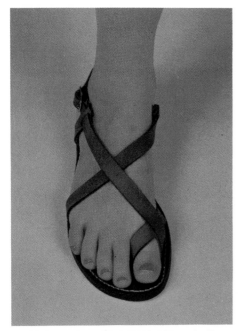

The Riviera sandal is designed for those who like a strap that encircles the big toe. The strap then crosses the instep, passes through ankle upright straps, and buckles at the outside ankle.

models, are placed at the ankle. To thread the toe strap, secure the strap under the sole at the base of the big toe. Bring the strap up to the top (Figure D), down at the inside big-toe slot, and up again at the outside big-toe slot. Cross the strap over the toe strap, and take it back to the outside ankle upright. Secure the second strap under the outside ball-of-the-foot slot, cross it over the other strap, and take it back to the inside ankle upright. Thread the straps through the slots in the ankle uprights and finish the sandal, following the directions on pages 1866 and 1867. To get the correct fit over the big toe, try on the sandal and adjust the straps as necessary. Mark the straps for buckle placement and attach the buckle.

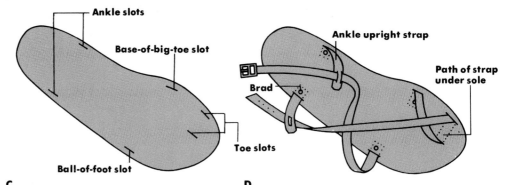

C
Figure C: Make the slots as shown in the sole for the Riviera sandal, with the two front slots moved in beside the big toe. The strap that is threaded through these slots will encircle that toe.

D
Figure D: The straps of the Riviera are anchored and threaded through the slots as shown. The dotted lines show the path of the strap underneath the sole.

Leathercrafts
The T-tie

$ 🗙 🧍 ⚗

Sandals that tie preceded the invention of the buckle. By lengthening straps, you can wind them around your leg as many times as you want, giving the sandal a timeless look. This T-tie sandal has a strap that starts at a slot at the inside of the big toe, and ends in a loop over the instep. You need one slot on the inside of the big toe and one on either side of the ankle (Figure E). A 12-inch-long strap is attached to the sole at the toe slot. The opposite end of this strap is riveted into a loop (Figure F). Long tie straps are threaded through the ankle slots, then through the loop, and are wrapped around your leg as many times as you like. The straps can be cut short and tied at the back of the ankle, or left long and wrapped up to your knee.

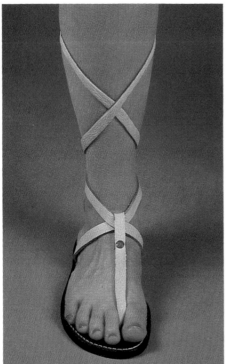

The T-tie sandal has 36-inch-long straps that can be wrapped around the calf and tied. Tie the straps in front or at the back, whichever is more comfortable.

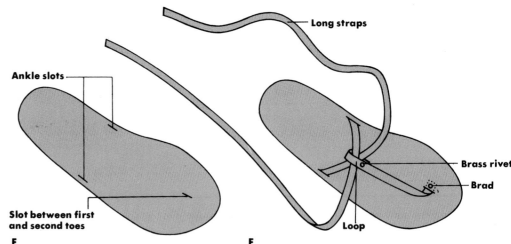

E
Figure E: To make the T-tie sandal, only three slots in the sole are needed—one for the toe strap, the other two for the ankle straps that wrap around the leg and tie.

F
Figure F: The straps of the T-tie sandal are threaded through the slots as shown; the short toe strap ends in a loop over the instep. Both ends of the ankle strap are threaded through this loop.

The blue-and-white needlepoint sandals below are the favorite footwear of the designer, Sandra Zubris. She also designed the needlepoint sandal at the left.

If you enjoy doing needlepoint, you can create a colorful sandal like this by making a needlepoint strap (Figure H, page 1870) and attaching it to a standard clog sole with screws.

Needlecrafts
Needlepoint clog sandals $ ⧖ ⚤ 🧵

One way to display your needlework talent is to make a pair of sandals combining splendid handmade straps with the ever-popular wooden clog soles. You can salvage the clogs from any worn-out pair, or you can purchase clog soles from the suppliers listed at right. The straps of the sandals can be needlepoint (as pictured above), or crewel embroidery, macramé, a narrow strip of weaving, or whatever your favorite needlecraft is, adapted to a 4-inch-wide strap 8½ inches long.

To make the sandals pictured, measure your instep to make sure that an 8½-inch strap will fit comfortably across your foot. If you need more room or less, simply add or subtract stitches to get the size you want. You will need: less than ¼ yard of 12-mesh needlepoint canvas (perhaps a piece left over from another project); less than ¼ yard of lightweight leather or medium-weight fabric for backing; a No. 20 tapestry needle; masking tape; tape measure; and sixteen ⅝-inch pan-head sheet metal screws. In the clogs pictured, yarn was used in the following amounts and colors: 1 yard each of rust, yellow, and dark turquoise; 2 yards each of rose, pink, and dark green; 3 yards each of gold, lavender, light blue, and dark blue; 4 yards each of red, purple, green, and turquoise; 5 yards each of lime, lemon, and orange; and 7 yards of white. You can choose your own colors, of course; this is a good place to use needlepoint yarn left over from other projects. Cut the canvas into two rectangles each 8 by 12½ inches (the dimensions of the finished needlepoint plus a 2-inch margin on each side). Bind the edges with masking tape to prevent raveling.

The Continental Stitch
The basic needlepoint stitch, called the tent stitch, covers one intersection of the canvas; it slants from lower left to upper right. When the stitch is worked in horizontal rows, it is called the continental stitch. To make this stitch, bring the needle and thread up from below to the left of the intersection to be covered. Bring the yarn across this intersection and go down above and to the right of it. Bring the needle up again in the hole directly to the left of the first hole (Figure G, page 1870). Continue across the row. For the second row, turn the canvas upside down and make the stitches directly above the first row (Figure G, bottom). Continue this way, turning the canvas at the end of each row. Follow Figure H for the design.

Sandra Zubris, who was graduated from the Rhode Island School of Design in 1969, moved to Cambridge, Massachusetts, where she spent several years painting and doing free-lance designing. Her work, exhibited in several art shows, resulted in her being commissioned to design needlework. Then she started her own designing firm, Zubris Needlepoint, in Cambridge, featuring her original hand-painted designs for needlepoint projects ranging in size from coasters to rugs.

Clog suppliers
Berman Leather Company
147 South Street
Boston, Mass. 02111

Just Brass Inc.
1612 Decatur Street
Ridgewood, N.Y. 11227

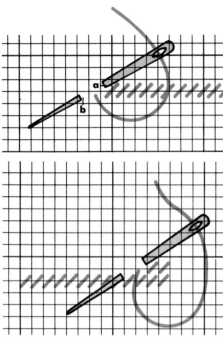

G

Figure G: To make a needlepoint continental stitch, take the needle down at *a* and bring it up at *b*. Repeat, making a row of stitches from right to left (top). To make the second row, also working from right to left, turn the canvas upside down (bottom). Continue working rows of continental stitches, turning the canvas at the end of each row.

H

Figure H: Each square in this grid represents one stitch on the needlepoint canvas. Follow this pattern using the colors you have chosen to make the needlepoint strap pictured on the sandal on page 1869.

32: Place the needlepoint strap on the clog sole where it feels most comfortable, and mark the placement of four screws on each side.

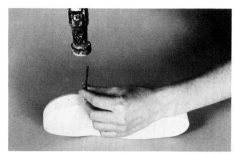

33: Using a hammer and nail, make a starting hole for each of the four screws you will drive on either side of the clog sole.

34: Make holes through the needlepoint with an awl so the screws do not tear it; then drive the screws in to hold the needlepoint in place.

Blocking

When your stitching is complete, it must be blocked. Blocking is done to smooth and straighten a finished needlepoint canvas that may have been stretched or pulled out of shape during stitching. You need: rustproof pushpins or tacks; a ¾-inch-thick piece of plywood larger than the worked needlepoint; brown wrapping paper; aluminum foil; a waterproof marker; a ruler; a T square or right-angled triangle; and a towel. Cover the board with aluminum foil. Place the brown wrapping paper on top of this. Using the waterproof marker, draw a rectangle the size that the finished needlepoint should be. Mark the center of each side on the paper and on the needlepoint. Soak the needlepoint; then roll tightly in a towel until the excess water is absorbed. Place the needlepoint face down on the paper, and tack the corners of the excess canvas to the board. Then tack the centers of each side, making sure the needlepoint marks and the rectangle on the paper line up. Continue placing tacks between previous tacks until they are ½ inch apart. Allow the needlepoint to dry completely, away from heat and sunlight.

Finishing

When the squared-up needlepoint is dry, trim the excess canvas to a ½-inch margin. Trace the same shape on lightweight leather or medium-weight fabric backing and cut it out. Place the needlepoint and backing with right sides together and machine stitch, ½ inch from the edge, leaving open what will be the inside edge (Figure I). Repeat with the strap for the other clog; then turn them both right side out and stitch the open sides closed, making small stitches by hand. To attach the straps to the soles, you need a hammer, a screwdriver, a nail, and an awl. Try on the clog, placing the needlepoint over your foot; mark the side of the sole for the placement of the screws (photograph 32). Remove the sandal and make four holes on each side of the sole, using a hammer and nail (photograph 33). With an awl, make four corresponding holes in each end of the needlepoint. Push the screws through the needlepoint and turn them into the holes in the clogs (photograph 34).

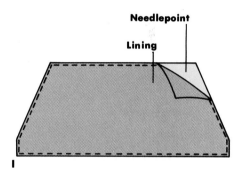

Needlepoint

Lining

I

Figure I: To attach the needlepoint to the lining, place both with right sides facing and stitch around three sides, leaving open the edge that will be tacked to the clog on the inside of the foot. Trim the seam, turn right side out, and stitch the opening closed by hand.

Needlecrafts
Ribbon clog sandals

$ ☒ 🧍 🧵

A quick way to make attractive sandals without taking time to create your own needlecraft is to use embroidered ribbon that you can buy. To make the sandals pictured (right), you will need: ½ yard of 2⅝-inch ribbon for the toe straps; 2 yards of ¾-inch ribbon for the ankle ties; and 16 upholsterer's tacks. Cut each piece of ribbon in half; you will use half the total for each sandal.

Try on the clog and decide where you want the strap to be. Mark this on the clog bottom. Determine how long you want the strap to be for your foot to fit comfortably; then fold the excess under on either end of the ribbon. Place the folded edge on the marked clog and hammer three tacks in each side to hold it in place. Then fold the narrow ribbon in half to determine its middle, and place this under the clog in the slope of the heel. Hammer in a tack on either side to keep the narrow ribbon in place; you will tie this ribbon over the instep to help hold the clog on your foot. Do the same with the other clog. If you want, you can line the ribbon (Figure I).

For related entries, see "Leather Working" and "Needlepoint."

A quick and easy way to make colorful sandals is to tack embroidered ribbons to a clog sole. The narrower ankle ribbons that are tied over the insteps keep the sandals on your feet.

Patricia Vardin has taught children at day care centers, in private preschools, public schools, and in summer programs. As head teacher of the Lathrop Learning Center at the YWCA, New York, Pat's emphasis is on integrating the creative arts into early childhood education. Members of her class are pictured on pages 1874 and 1875. Pat is also an assistant professor at the State University of New York at New Paltz, and a doctoral candidate at The Teachers College of Columbia University, New York.

Janyce Jeffreys teaches candle making at the Crafts Students League in New York and at her home on Long Island. Always interested in the arts, Janyce studied ballet and piano in Oregon, (where she spent her childhood), in New York, and in Paris. She also works in stained glass, calligraphy, and sculpture. Her candle is on page 1875.

Jolyon Hofsted, former director of the Brooklyn Museum Art School, Brooklyn, New York, is the author of Ceramics and Pottery. *His work is represented at the Museum of Contemporary Crafts, New York; the Museum of Modern Art, Kyoto, Japan; and the Brooklyn Museum, where he had an 11-year retrospective of his work. Among the many exhibitions of his work is one at the Distinguished Contemporary Potters Invitational Creative Arts Workshop in New Haven, Connecticut. Jolyon created the weed pot on page 1878.*

SAND CASTING
Shaped by True Grit

Sand casting is an art form in which soft plaster or other molding material is poured into a mold made of damp sand, for the specific purpose of having the casting, as it hardens, pick up and hold a layer of sand on its surface. The resulting sand casting has a primitive look, although the technique of sand casting originated as part of a precise method of duplicating machine components. In the industrial application, molten bronze is poured into molds cut in fine black sand to produce gears for machinery. But in the art application of sand casting, the very lack of precision and the spontaneity of the designs that result are appealing aspects.

There are two kinds of sand that can be used for sand casting—beach sand and commercial sand. Beach sand, available along the shore of almost any lake or ocean, is relatively coarse and full of contaminants like pebbles, shells, seaweed, and twigs. So if you have access to beach sand and want to use it for sand casting, pick through the sand first (or sift it) to remove the larger foreign matter. This coarse sand will give a rough texture to your sand casting. Commercial sand, washed and sifted, is available at hardware stores and building-supply houses; it is fine and even sand with no contaminants, not even the salt that is in ocean-beach sand. If you buy this sand, you can use it as it comes, and your casting will have a fine, even texture. Colored sand, available at pet stores and plant stores, can be used to accent the casting if some of it is mixed into the surface layer of your mold.

To make either type of sand into a mold, you need to add enough water to dampen the sand until it retains its shape when a handful is squeezed together, yet is not so wet that it will not hold an impression.

Sand casting offers a great range of projects; it can be simple enough for kindergarteners or sophisticated enough to interest an accomplished craftsman. The first two projects that follow show a two-step method of casting. First, a group of children make a mold in sand, then pour plaster of paris into the mold to make wall hangings, and second, a candlemaker makes a sand mold and pours in melted wax to make a sand-coated candle. The third project involves a three-step method; a potter makes a mound of sand on which he pours plaster, thus making a plaster mold that he then uses to shape a clay pot.

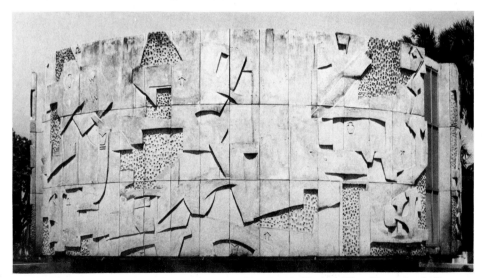

To create the sand-casted panels for this library in Miami Beach, Florida, Albert Vrana first built frames to the exact measurement of each panel. He used dry sand to make the mold, poured dry cement on top, then hosed it all down with water. The surface hardened to create the patterns shown.

Jolyon Hofsted puts finishing touches on a sand-casted pot, traditionally used to display interesting weeds. It was cast from the plaster mold visible at its right. Directions for the pot begin on page 1878.

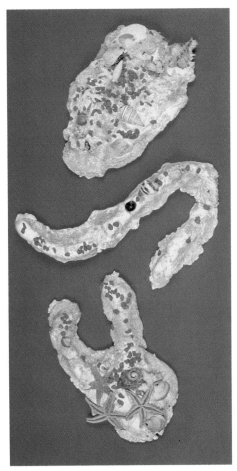

Beach babies created by the children in Pat Vardin's preschool class include a clam (top), an eel (center), and a crab (bottom). The plaster castings are decorated with shells and pebbles.

1: In the damp sand, a child draws an outline of the shape that he wants to cast. Following the beach theme, the children drew fish and other creatures of the sea.

2: In an exercise in three-dimensional imagination, this young artist removes sand from inside the shape that he drew so he can fill the negative image with plaster.

Carving and Molding
Beach babies

If you have ever watched children playing at the beach, you have seen how their creativity is stimulated by such simple, natural things as sand and shells. But children do not have to live near a beach to enjoy such activity. In fact, the children in a preschool class in New York simulated a beach by filling disposable foil baking pans with sand. They were given colored pebbles and shells, available at variety stores, to use in decorating the molds. First, the children dampened the sand by adding water to it. When the sand held its shape, each child drew an outline in the sand of the object he or she wanted to create (photograph 1). The class created beach babies—fish and other creatures of the sea. The child removed sand from the outlined shape to form a convex mold that would hold liquid plaster of paris (photograph 2). Then he decorated the molds with shells and brightly colored pebbles (photograph 3), and poured plaster into the mold (photograph 4). After the plaster had been allowed to set for 24 hours, the child removed his casting and brushed away loose sand. The results are pictured above (left). A detail of the surface with the sand and shells adhering to the plaster is shown opposite. If you help a child with such a project, do not mix the plaster ahead of time; wait until he is ready to use it. Following package directions, mix dry plaster of paris and water in a plastic container until the desired consistency is reached. Do not continue to mix; this hastens the hardening process. To clean up later, squeeze the container and the hardened plaster will pop out.

3: The decorative shells and colored pebbles that will appear on the outside of the casting must be carefully arranged inside the mold, face down, of course.

4: Plaster the consistency of heavy cream is poured into the hollowed-out shape. Then there is nothing to do but wait—for 24 hours at least— before removing the creation for all to admire.

A close-up view of one of the sand-casted beach babies (shown in their entirety on the opposite page) shows how the sand, shells, and pebbles adhere to the surface of the plaster.

Carving and Molding
Sand-casted candle $ ◪ 👫 ♨

To make sand-casted candles, you need: wax and a wick for the candle; sand; a container for the sand; a container for the wax; and a means of melting the wax. A wooden box, such as an old milk-bottle container, is ideal for holding the sand, but you can use a plastic container if you make sure the hot wax will not touch the plastic. With a plastic container, put a flat piece of wood on the bottom to make sure that the bottom of your cast candle will be flat.

As a container for the candle wax while it is being melted, an old coffee pot works well because it has a built-in spout and an insulated handle. You also could use a 3-pound coffee can bent at the top edge to form a lip for pouring. But if you do use the coffee can, be sure to wear asbestos gloves while handling it. Melted wax is not only hot, it is flammable. For safety's sake, tie your hair back and wear a smock. Have a fire extinguisher on hand—the kind designed to put out grease fires. Salt or sand can also be used to smother flaming melted wax.

Wax, candle color, and wicks are sold at craft supply stores. You will learn from experience how to estimate the amount of wax you need for any given candle, but as a general guide, a ten-pound slab of raw wax will make four quart-sized candles.

Candlewicks used for sand-casted candles are made of cotton yarn braided around wire and are sold in spools in three weights—thin, medium, and thick. The candle, right, has a medium wick. Large candles require heavy wicks; thin tapers need thin wicks.

This sand-casted candle has a shell windbreaker, (which was placed in the mold before the wax was poured), sculptured sand sides, and bits of brown wax melted decoratively on top.

5: Make your sand candle in a container that will not leak sand. Pack the damp sand as compactly as you can; then level the top.

6: Make a hole the shape the candle is to be, using your hand or a container as a scoop. Smooth the top edges and brush away loose sand.

7: Position the windbreak shell along one edge by pushing it gently against the sand until it sticks in the right place.

8: Pour melted wax slowly and carefully into the hole. Do not let it splatter; the wax is very hot and can cause painful burns.

9: Immediately after you pour wax into the hole, lift up the shell to let the melted wax run behind the shell.

10: Put the shell back in position so it will adhere to the wax as it hardens. Note how the hot wax is soaking into the sand at the edges.

Other tools for sand-casting candles include: a candy or wax thermometer; a hammer for breaking slabs of wax into small pieces; a stick for stirring the wax when you mix colors; a piece of heavy wire or an ice pick to use as a wick inserter; a small brush for removing excess sand; a broad knife or putty knife for scraping sand off; an inexpensive set of wood-carving tools for sculpting; safety goggles; and a small propane torch for torching and melding the sand into the wax.

The sand in the box should be a bit deeper than the height of the candle. In this project, a 5-inch candle is made; so the sand needs to be about 6 inches deep. This gives the candle as level a bottom as possible. Moisten the sand enough to make it hold a shape when you form a ball. If drops of moisture appear on the surface, add dry sand. Pack down the sand as solidly as you can with your hands; then level the top evenly (photograph 5). Make the mold the shape you want by forming a hole and scooping out the excess sand carefully. The bottom of the hole should be about 1 inch from the bottom of the container. Pack the sand in the hole as solidly as you can, refining the shape of the mold with your hands (photograph 6). Then brush loose sand away from the top and smooth the edges.

If you like, position a clam shell or piece of driftwood on one edge by pushing it into the side of the sand mold (photograph 7). You also could use stones, bits of colored glass, or glass jewels by pressing the pieces into the sides just far enough so they will protrude slightly from the finished candle. The mold is now ready to receive the melted wax.

Heat the wax to 250 degrees Fahrenheit (but never hotter than 290 degrees, since hot wax is combustible). Add color at this point and stir it in with a stick. Then pour the wax slowly and carefully into the sand mold (photograph 8). Immediately, lift the shell to let the wax flow behind it (photograph 9); then replace the shell (photograph 10). This will help attach the shell to the finished candle. In a few minutes, the wax will soak into the sand, as you can see in photograph 10. Add more melted wax until you reach the brim of the mold. In 10 or 15 minutes, an indentation will form in the center of the candle. Again, add melted wax until the mold is filled. Let the candle cool for one to three hours.

An air pocket will form at the center of the candle. To puncture it, heat an ice pick or a heavy wire, and push it into the center of the pocket (photograph 11). The middle of the candle will sink slightly. Fill again with melted wax (photograph 12).

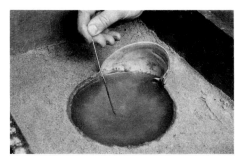

11: To puncture the air pocket that has formed after several hours of cooling, heat a piece of wire and poke the center. It will sink slightly.

12: Fill the sunken center of the candle with more melted wax. The air pocket may have to be punctured and filled more than once.

13: After the candle has cooled for 24 hours, remove it from the sand by digging gently around it. Invert it and let it cool for another 24 hours.

14: Make a hole for the wick with a heated length of wire or ice pick, poking in a bit at a time; then quickly insert the wick into the hole.

15: To sculpt the outside of the candle, heat it lightly with the propane torch; then cut out your pattern with a heated wood-carving tool.

16: To decorate the top of the sand candle, drop bits of brown wax on top and soften them slightly with the torch.

Indeed, the air pocket may have to be filled several times. Be sure to test it with the ice pick or wire because this air pocket, if left in the candle, could cause the wick to collapse when the candle is lit. Leave the candle in the sand to harden for about 24 hours. Then remove it from the box by gently digging up the sand around it (photograph 13). Trim the top edge smooth with a knife, and brush away any excess sand that clings to the bottom. Turn the candle upside down and let it dry for another 24 hours. The candle must be thoroughly dry before you do more work on it. Larger candles will need even more time to dry.

When the candle is dry, insert the wick. First measure the candle with a ruler. The wick should extend from 1 inch above the bottom of the candle to ½ inch above the top. Heat a wick-puncher—either a piece of wire or an ice pick—as you hold it with an insulated glove. Use the heated punch to make the wick hole, going straight down in the center of the candle. Do not force the wick-puncher or you might crack the candle; reheat it if necessary. Remove the wick-puncher and insert the wick quickly into the hole (photograph 14).

Torching is a process of melding sand into the wax, using a small propane torch as a heat source so loose sand will not fall from the candle. You can simply torch the outside, sweeping the flame lightly and quickly over the sides of the candle, being careful not to ignite the wax. Or you can actually sculpt the sides with the aid of the torch, making interesting patterns in the sand. Wearing safety goggles, heat the tip of a tool from the wood-carving set using the torch flame. Prop the candle so the area you want to work on is on top. Torch the sand lightly and start carving. The sand can be pared away easily if it is heated and the carving tool is hot (photograph 15). You can work on one area again and again until you are satisfied with the results. But don't trust to luck; have a pattern in mind before you begin to carve. Wherever you scrape away sand so the wax is exposed, light from the candle flame will show through. Various finishes and textures can be obtained by using the torch to smooth out edges of areas that have been dug out, by leaving them rough and unfinished, or by making deep indentations with a knife. Being constantly aware of the fire danger, make sure all the sand is melded into the wax. Finish the top of the candle by first torching it lightly, then sprinkling shavings of a contrasting colored wax on top. Soften some of these small pieces so the two colors of wax are blended (photograph 16).

Carving and Molding
Weed pot

Making a sand-casted pot of clay like the one at left (called a weed pot because its narrow neck accommodates tall thin weeds and shows them off to their best advantage), involves an intermediary step between the mold of damp sand and the clay—a mold made of plaster of paris. This second mold lets you duplicate the shape many times. You can make many bowls from one mold, for example, or you can put two matching halves together, add a neck piece, and make a pot, as is done in this project. You will need sand, plaster of paris, and potter's clay. Any kind of potter's clay can be used for sand casting, but how the pot is finished will be determined by the kind of clay chosen.

The temperature of the kiln (the oven used for firing and thus hardening pottery) and the type of glaze (the thin layer of clear or colored glass that is melted on the surface to add color and make the pot watertight) are determined by the clay used. The pot shown at the left, made of a high-fired stoneware clay mixed by the potter, was fired in a kiln at Cone 4 temperature and was glazed with a Cone 4 blue glaze. When you buy potter's clay, the firing range is indicated on the package by cone numbers; pyrometric cones are placed inside a kiln before firing and their melting indicates the temperature reached. If you take your pot to a commercial kiln to be fired, be sure to specify the firing range of the clay.

The Sand Mold
The first step is to make a shaped sand mold slightly larger than you want the finished pot to be (photograph 17). Clay shrinks about ten percent as it dries and is fired. Use sand damp enough to hold its shape. In this case you are making a positive image of the finished pot, rather than a reversed negative image as in earlier projects. So sculpt the surface of the sand mound until it looks as you want the pot to look, using a paint stirrer, a spatula, and other household tools. Just make sure there are no undercuts in the mold that would interfere with later steps (photograph 18). The sand mold is now ready for the plaster. Using a plastic bucket, follow the package instructions as you add the plaster to the water. Always use fresh plaster; plaster that has been opened, then stored, picks up moisture and will not harden properly. You want a thin, watery mix at the start. Add handfuls of plaster by sifting it in through your fingers. Never stir the plaster. When an island of plaster forms in the middle of the bucket, the plaster is ready to mix. (If you coat your hands with petroleum jelly before working with plaster, you can remove the plaster from your hands as soon as you finish by running cold water over them, thus minimizing the danger that the plaster might irritate your skin.) With your hand stretched open flat, mix the plaster quickly and just enough to get all the lumps out (photograph 19). If you want the plaster to set up quickly, add salt to the plaster-and-water mixture. If you want the plaster to set up slowly to give you more time to work, add vinegar to the mixture. The next step is to get the plaster onto the sand mold without marring any of the details. You have to be careful not to trap air bubbles between sand and plaster. Dribble the plaster on sparingly with your hand in what is called a splatter coat (photograph 20). This first layer is the critical part of the mold; the rest of the plaster is added simply for reinforcement. When the sand mold is covered with the splatter coat, dribble on thicker plaster— the plaster thickens as time passes (photograph 21). Let this layer of plaster harden. (If you are making a large form, you can guard against cracks by dipping burlap into the plaster and laying it over the wet plaster mold for reinforcement.) Wait for the plaster to dry; adding more plaster before the plaster has dried would weaken the mold. When the plaster mold is hard, swirl on the final coat (photograph 22). Before this plaster sets up and becomes too hard to cut, trim the edge clean with a knife (photograph 23). When the plaster has completely cured (a chemical action that may take up to a week depending on the humidity), dig the sand out from around the base of the plaster mold, and lift the mold off the sand mound (photograph 24). Hose out the inside of the mold to get rid of any loose sand (photograph 25), let it dry, and the mold is ready to receive the clay.

This sand-casted clay weed pot was coated with a blue glaze and fired in a kiln. The result: an unusual container for dried weeds and seed pods.

17: To make a clay pot with a sand mold, start by making a shaped mound of damp sand slightly larger than you want half the finished pot to be.

18: Using a paint stirrer, spatula, and other household tools, sculpt and texture the sand surface until you are pleased with the design.

19: Use your open hand to mix the plaster into the water until all lumps of plaster are dissolved, but do not stir the mix.

20: Splatter the plaster sparingly onto the sand mound so you preserve all details without getting air bubbles between sand and plaster.

21: When the sand is covered with the splatter coat, carefully dribble on more plaster to make the cast thicker.

22: After the coat of plaster on the sand mold has hardened, swirl on a final thick coat of plaster to serve as reinforcement.

23: Before the final coat of plaster hardens completely, trim around the edge of the mold evenly with a knife.

24: When the plaster mold has dried thoroughly (perhaps as much as a week later), carefully lift it off the sand mound.

25: Wash out any loose sand from the inside of the plaster mold, using a hose adjusted to give a gentle spray of water.

26: Place a ½-inch-thick slab of potter's clay into the mold and gently push it in. A single slab works better than pieced slabs.

27: Add more clay to raise any internal depressions caused by the mold, and push hard enough for the clay to take on the shape of the mold.

28: To pick up the texture of the sand that is in the plaster mold, go over the clay carefully, inch by inch, with your fingertips.

29: To reinforce the edge that will be the joint between the pot halves, add a plump roll of clay all around the edge.

30: Ease the clay back from the edge of the mold slightly to let air enter. This will speed the drying of the clay.

31: When the clay has dried to a leather hardness (about 15 minutes), flip it out of the mold onto a board.

32: Leave the clay on the board, and put it in the sun to dry further while you make the second half of the pot.

33: While the two halves are drying, make a neck for the pot by pushing a slab of clay into the mold to pick up sand texture.

Working with Clay

Roll out a slab of potter's clay ½ inch thick and large enough to cover the entire mold in one piece. Using one large slab of clay rather than piecing small ones together makes a smoother pot. Place the slab of clay in the mold and gently push it down (photograph 26). Then add more clay to fill depressions and pack it in against the mold (photograph 27). Go over the entire mold, pressing down with your fingertips inch by inch so the clay picks up all the texture of the mold (photograph 28). Then smooth the inside of the clay, and add a thick roll of clay around the edge to serve as reinforcement when you take the clay out of the mold and when you join the two halves (photograph 29). Ease the clay inward a bit all around the edge, so air can get down into the mold and make the clay dry faster (photograph 30). If the plaster mold was completely dry before you added the clay, the clay will dry to leather hardness in about 15 minutes in the sun. Then place a board on top of the mold (photograph 31), turn board and mold over, and flip the clay out (photograph 32). Starting with the plaster mold, make the second half of the pot exactly the same way, and flip it, too, out on a board to dry.

While the two halves are drying in the sun, make a neck for the pot. Push a slab of clay into part of the mold so the neck will pick up the same texture as the pot (photo-

34: When the neck clay has the texture of the mold so it matches the pot, roll the ends together to make a tube.

35: Press the ends of the rolled clay slab together carefully where they meet to form the neck for the clay pot.

36: Using a craft knife, scratch nicks into the edges of both halves of the pot. This is called scoring the edges.

37: Put slip, a thin mixture of clay and water used to cement the halves, on the scored edges of both halves.

38: Join the two halves and add more slip, smoothing the joint so the halves meet exactly, without any gaps.

39: When the joint is smooth, rub sand into the fresh slip so it will have the same texture as the rest of the pot.

40: With a craft knife, cut a hole slightly larger than the neck piece in what will become the top of the pot.

41: Put the neck piece into the hole at the top, adding slip to secure the joining. When the slip dries, the pot is ready for kiln firing.

graph 33). Then lift the ends of the clay from the mold so you can roll it (photograph 34), pressing the ends together to join them (photograph 35). Let the neck piece dry in the sun.

When the neck has dried to a leather hardness, the pot is ready to assemble. Make a nest in the sand to hold the pot so it doesn't collapse as you are working on it. Using a craft knife, score the edge of both halves of the pot (photograph 36). Then put slip, a liquid mixture of clay and water used to cement the two halves together, along the scored edges of both halves (photograph 37). Put the two halves together and add as much more slip as you need to make a smooth joint (photograph 38). When the joint is smooth and secure, rub sand over the slip so the joint has the same texture as the rest of the pot (photograph 39). Using a craft knife, cut a hole in what will be the top of the pot (photograph 40). Make the hole slightly larger than the circumference of the neck piece. Put the neck into the hole in the pot (photograph 41), using slip to cement the joint. When the slip is dry, the pot is ready to be taken to a kiln to be bisque-fired, the first firing that strengthens the leather-hard pot so it is safer to handle during glazing. The bisque-fired pot is then ready to be glazed and given a final firing.

For related entries, see "Casting," "Molding Methods," and "Pottery."

The Kidwells sculpted and painted their prize-winning Sesame Street Muppet characters (top) using ordinary household tools such as a spatula and an old knife. They worked on the face of a sand mound angled at 45 degrees for good display. The lower picture shows work in progress on Big Bird for the Sand Castle Carnival. To make the dry pigments stick to the sand, keep moistening the area of the design to be colored.

SAND CHARACTERS AND CASTLES
An Ephemeral Art Form

The softness of dry sand filtering through fingers and toes plus the plasticity of cool, wet sand near the water appeal to the touch of adults as well as children. On any beach day, even the tiniest of tots at play along the shore will be building dams and dikes of wet sand or digging holes and tunnels to trap water, making moats for fairy-tale castles. Sand modeling, an advanced form of such sand play, shown in the photographs opposite and on pages 1884, 1885, 1886, and 1887, involves molding, carving, and decorating designs on a large scale. There is something wonderfully carefree about building an elaborate and totally useless design that will be gone with the next incoming tide. Like the jazz performance that goes unrecorded or the calypso verses that are not transcribed, the joy is in the doing.

Special Events
The designs pictured were entered in a competition in Fort Lauderdale, Florida, for residents of Broward County. This springtime spectacle on South Beach was sponsored jointly by the Fort Lauderdale Recreation Department and the Fort Lauderdale News. Such sand crafting is popular in many beach communities throughout the world. If you aspire to be a participant, the Chamber of Commerce or Tourist Bureau near any beach can tell you if a sand modeling event is scheduled.

Design Fundamentals
If you would like to create an original sand model for fun or competition, first make several rough sketches of subjects that require little detail. Be sure each part of the composition is in scale with other parts. Simple, easy-to-recognize subjects such as fairy-tale characters or cartoon animals tend to be popular, since viewers of any age can identify these. For greater animation, you can sculpt the characters in motion. For example, one character in the top photograph, opposite, is bobbing out of a garbage can; a balloon tied to the lid is soaring into space; the man holds a paint can and paintbrush; the big bird appears to be strutting and squawking.

Control of the wet sand's consistency is essential in sand sculpture. Various modeling tools such as boards, shovels, and old kitchen utensils will help you pack it and shape it to achieve realistic effects. Water-soluble paints in vibrant colors plus beach-combing finds such as seaweed or shells can be used to decorate the design. Too, visibility of the completed design contributes to its success. One way to increase visibility is to elevate the design by building it on top of a mound of sand. Three types of mounding are described on page 1886.

How Sand Is Made
A close look at a handful of sand reveals tiny, gritty, multihued particles that were once part of such natural formations as coral reefs and volcanic rocks. Ocean beach sand is formed by the turbulent pounding of the surf. Eventually the lightest and finest particles—silt and clay as well as sand—come to rest at the water's edge. Sand can also be found along inland lakes and rivers, of course, and such sand, formed as water freezes and thaws in rock crevices, is likely to be grittier than ocean beach sand because it has not been polished smooth by the surf. This sharpness of inland sand is an advantage in sand modeling, but then, so is the saltiness of ocean sand; so either will work well.

Preparations
Before you begin to model a large patch of beach sand such as the 10-by-10-foot plot shown opposite, pinpoint the time of high and low tide by consulting a tide chart, the local weather bureau, a newspaper, or the coast guard. Use this information to determine the amount of time you have available to finish your design before it is swept away. On a bright or hazy day, wear a hat and a T-shirt for protection from the sun, and don't forget the sun-tan lotion. If you plan to erect a mound on which to model a design, you will need a spade, buckets, two 16-inch

Barbara and Jack Kidwell and their children, Gina, Keith, and Marty, live in Fort Lauderdale, Florida. For three years in a row, they won first prize in the family division of the Fort Lauderdale Sand Carnival for their beach-sculpture interpretations of fairy-tale and cartoon characters. Barbara is a homemaker, den mother, Girl Scout leader, and Sunday school teacher. Jack manages a cooperative for dairy farmers in southeast Florida.

This Mayan pyramid was modeled from a low pile of wet sand, then painted. The designer, a contestant in the adult division of the Fort Lauderdale contest, painstakingly carved each step of the terraces and stairs. Flat sticks were used as modeling tools.

What is a sand carnival without a castle? This design, entered in the adult division, presents an imaginative, crenellated castle protected by a wide moat. Small tools such as ice cream sticks can be used to scoop out arches and windows without cracking the sand walls.

Ted Melnick and Annette De Luca, students at Broward Community College, modeled this larger-than-life couple sun-bathing by the shore. They used their hands as sculpting tools. The knee of the female bather was raised by modeling the knee in the round and supporting it on a low mound of sand.

wooden 2-by-4s, and a watering can. In addition to ocean water, some modelers add water-soluble glue or rock salt to the moist sand to keep the molded forms from crumbling as they dry out, but such additives should be used only where the builder can be certain they will all be washed completely away. Your hands are the most valuable tools for modeling large forms, but you will find other implements helpful for detailed work: packers (a pair of large flat boards); cutters (knifelike pieces of wood); tamps (wood spatulas); and points (long thin sticks, sharp on one end and flat on the other). Other tools found about the house that can be used to create various surface effects are old knives, cookie cutters, spatulas, potato mashers, putty knives, and trowels. You can add color to your design with powdered poster paints, calcimine colors, spray paint, or plastic applicators filled with liquid tempera paints. Natural materials such as shells, seaweed, stones, and palm leaves are often used for finishing details. A small can of turpentine and a rag should be kept on hand to remove tar from hands and feet. Then pack a towel and all of your materials in a large beach bag with a picnic lunch and refreshments.

Readying the Sand

To begin, choose a sand plot and remove all extraneous materials (such as shells, seaweed, tar, and driftwood) with a fine-toothed rake or a hoe with a mesh scooper (an attachment used for cleaning up beaches). At least one hour before you start to build your mound, pour several large buckets of salt water on the dry surface sand, continuing until the sand is saturated. Use a spade or a large shovel to turn the sand over so it is moist throughout, digging at least 10 inches deep or until you reach sand that is naturally wet. To determine when the sand has reached the proper working consistency, put a small amount in the palm of your hand and make a fist. If your fingerprints remain embedded in the sand, it is ready to be modeled.

This fierce sea turtle, painstakingly modeled from a low, flat mound of sand, was an entry in the teen-age division of the Fort Lauderdale contest—that is a fish dangling from the turtle's mouth. Low subjects such as this that can be treated as bas-relief sculpture are the most successful.

Mounds

The television characters shown on page 1882 were modeled on a 4-foot-high mound with the top slanted at a 45-degree angle. Such a mound is effective when used for low-relief modeling because it tilts the design upward for more comfortable viewing. To build such an angled mound, wet down the sand; then use a shovel to dig a trench in the front one-third of the sand plot. Dig about two feet deep and pile the sand on the back of the plot, as high as you want the tallest part of the design to be. Then use your hands to shape and smooth the top and side edges of the pile. With a packer board in each hand, push and press the sand hard until the top surface of the mound forms a smooth angled face, as in the design on page 1882. Draw an enlarged version of your sketch on the face of the mound, using a pointed modeling tool such as an old knife or a pointed stick (photograph 1). Then sculpt the design.

Also popular among sand crafters is flat modeling. The beagle puppy at left and

1: On the smooth surface of the wet sand mound, outline the design you have planned for your sand modeling, using a pointed tool.

2: Rock salt stirred into the sand will help to keep it from drying out too rapidly and getting crumbly as you work.

A contestant in the teen-age category modeled this beagle puppy in sand—giving him a very relaxed stance as befits the wet-sand medium. The form of the dog was gradually built up and smoothed by hand from the tip of his wagging tail to his slurping tongue.

3: To raise areas of low relief, pack moist sand into a ball and press it into place over the sketch. Then shape it with your hands.

4: You can also carve sand away along the edges of a design so it stands out in greater relief against the flat surface of the mound.

the sun-bathers on page 1884 were made this way. For flat modeling, use packers or a tamp to press the wet sand until you have a smooth, compact, level surface. Then use a pointed tool such as the edge of a shell to outline your design. Fill in the outline with wet sand, and use your hands to round and smooth the contours until the relief sculpture is as high as you wish.

Modeling in the round is the most common way of shaping objects. This technique was used to make the Mayan pyramid and the castle on page 1884. To model in the round, pile sand until you have a mound similar in shape and size to the object you are depicting. Then use your hands or a cutter tool to slice and carve the mound until it approximates the shape you need. All sand sculptures tend to be squat, since any overhanging edge would quickly crumble away, and even vertical surfaces are hard to keep uncracked.

Modeling and Decorating

Once the mound is smooth and the general shape of the design has been indicated on its surface, you are ready to do detailed molding and carving. If you are sculpting on a mound, use moist sand from the bottom of the trench in front. Small amounts of rock salt added to the sand will help to keep it moist and compact (photograph 2). Knead the sand to make it more pliable, and stick small lumps (about the size of a softball) onto the sketch to raise areas of relief a bit at a time (photograph 3). Or with your hands or a spatula, you can carve away sand along the outer edges of the molded design to make it appear higher against the background of the mound (photograph 4). In addition to adding salt, to keep the sand from drying out and crumbling as you work, you will need to keep sprinkling the molded forms with a watering can as the surface sand dries (photograph 5).

As your work progresses, shape the detailed contours of the design with improvised tools. An ice-cream stick was used to carve zigzag and scalloped details of the sculpture on page 1882, adding the contrast of texture and shadow. When you finish modeling one part of the design, use the watering can to moisten adjacent surfaces before continuing.

Use packers—a pair of flat boards—to shape parallel rows. A tool with a straight edge (such as a spatula) is useful in defining and sharpening edges even

5: Keep a watering can handy—you will need it to keep the surface of the sand moist as your work progresses.

6: To establish sharp outlines for a linear pattern, use a tool with a straight edge (such as a spatula or the edge of a board).

7: When you spray a water-based paint onto a large area, use a board as a windbreak to keep the paint mist from drifting.

8: A plastic applicator bottle filled with liquid tempera paint can be used to draw in fine details, such as these thin lines around the eyes.

There is nothing to stop you from building a sand castle the old-fashioned way, using a pail for a mold. Fill the pail with moist sand, invert it, tap it to loosen the sand, and you have a castle tower. Shells and stones still make very satisfactory decorations.

more (photograph 6). Metal or plastic molds, such as those used for baking or gelling liquids, are handy when you want to add a repetitive surface pattern. To do this, fill the mold with moist sand and position it where the pattern is needed. Then shake the mold gently to release the sand.

Painting the Sculpture

If paint is to adhere to the sand, the molded areas must be kept moist. A water-based paint, sprayed on, can be used for large areas requiring only one color. If the wind is blowing (as it often is at the shore) have someone hold a wide board between you and the wind while you spray. The board will act as a windbreak to keep the paint where it belongs (photograph 7). Sprinkling dry tempera paint colors over damp sand is a good way to apply color to small areas without making a mess. To outline parts of the design so they contrast with colored areas, use a plastic applicator bottle filled with liquid tempera paint. You can draw thin lines and guide the paint flow by squeezing the container (photograph 8). You can improve eyes with painted seashells, hair with seaweed. For a finished look, smooth the trench area with the packers.

For related entries, see "Pottery" and "Sculpture."

SAND PAINTING AND LAYERING
Ancient Ritual to Home Terrarium

A twilight sky can be layered in brightly colored sand, effective in a broad, shallow, open planter. Conveniently for the sand painter, the swans are depicted preening themselves rather than stretching their necks upward to the sky.

Philip Perl is a writer who was born in Manhattan and educated at Columbia University. He was on the staff of The New Yorker *magazine for 20 years, and is now a sand painter at Terrarium Town in New York, where he also teaches the art. He is the author of* The Sandpainting Book.

Sand paintings have been found in every arid region, from the Gobi Desert of Mongolia to the Mohave Desert of the United States. Its practitioners have ranged from Tibetans who lived centuries ago to members of a dozen contemporary American Indian tribes, most notably the Navahos of the Southwest.

Navaho Sand Paintings

A Navaho sand painting is made primarily with the naturally colored sands that abound in the region inhabited by the tribe. Indeed, these sands, in colors ranging from purple to pink, make the entire area look like a magnificent—and permanent—sand painting. Unfortunately, those created by the Navahos are more ephemeral; they are destroyed almost immediately after they are created by the Navahos themselves.

The reason is itself interesting. To the Navaho, the sand painting is not created as a thing of beauty but as a utilitarian curative agent. When a Navaho is stricken with illness, the men of the tribe, working under the direction of a medicine man, prepare sand paintings of the spirits with power over illnesses. In addition to colored sand, just about anything else that comes to hand and provides color may be added to the painting, such as ground charcoal, powdered seeds and grains, and crushed rocks. These are sprinkled on the ground in strokes that make portraits of the Navaho spirits being invoked. The patient is seated in the center of the completed painting, and the entire tribe assembles around it. A chant that will continue for days is begun to urge the patient on in his struggle with the illness.

When the painting is judged to have done its job, it is dismantled. Some say its components, now contaminated, must be scattered to the far corners of the land; others say handfuls of the sand are taken for luck by the chanters. In either case, the painting is destroyed. Fortunately, a few scholars have persuaded the Navahos to permit photographs of the art, and some Indians, David Villaseñor among them, have published collections of their own sand paintings. The example shown on page 1890 first appeared, together with many other designs, in his book, *Tapestries in Sand: The Spirit of Indian Sandpainting.*

Monument Valley, Utah, a landscape in layered sand, embellishes a terrarium. You can brighten any transparent container with scenes like this, working with improvised tools and using dyed sand that is commercially available.

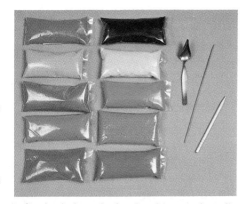

1: Sand painting, whether done in two or three dimensions, requires dyed sand. It is available in dozens of hues at plant and terrarium stores. You also need a few tools that can be improvised. Above, top to bottom, are an old spoon with sides bent up with pliers to control the flow of sand, a knitting needle, and a dowel sharpened to a point at one end.

Paint and Color
A desert sand painting

You can do a two-dimensional sand painting based on the Navaho art, using simple tools and materials (photograph 1, page 1889). But instead of the earth, use a sheet of particle board, plywood, or illustration board as the base. It can be any size you want. In many places, natural materials can be collected and used for sand painting. Otherwise, use dyed sands (available in dozens of hues at garden centers) and spices from the kitchen.

Techniques
Draw a design on the base board with chalk or crayon. You could use the sand painting below as an inspiration, but the Navahos, when they adapt motifs from a sand painting for use in a tapestry or rug, are careful to alter at least one detail, thus avoiding sacrilege.

Cover the base board completely and evenly with a slow-drying household glue, such as mucilage or wheat paste. Spoon the sand onto the glued surface a bit at a time, keeping the various colors within the outlines of the design. With a blunt stick or a small paintbrush, spread the sand over each section. Use small amounts of sand until you can guess what volume of sand will cover a given area of base board. To pour sand in thin lines, bend the sides of an old spoon into a pouring spout with pliers. There is no reason to let the sand accumulate to any depth; only a thin layer will stick. If you want to create a limited third dimension, you can spread glue evenly in low-relief patterns, or, once the glue has dried, you can add more glue and sand over the original layer.

Cactus Sandpainting With Blossoms, by David Villaseñor, is an authentic example of the sacred art of Indian sand painting. Designs like this one are used in mystical healing ceremonies.

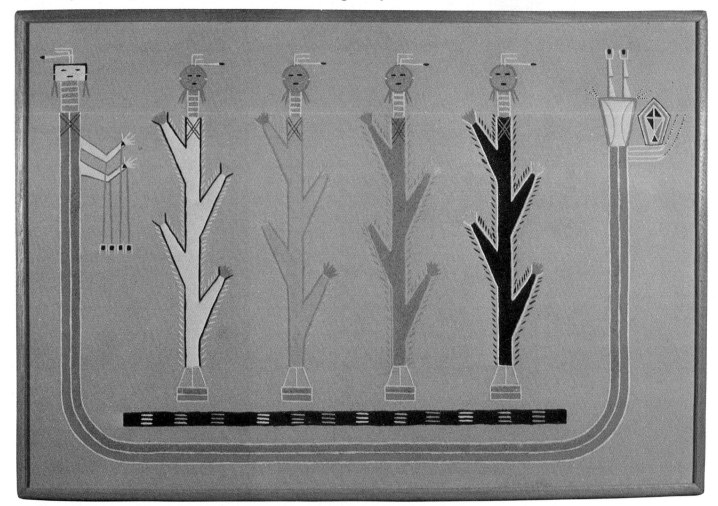

The Navahos usually work on a pastel background and use bright colors sparingly. Although color areas traditionally are sharply delineated, you can blend tones if you like by feathering the sand lightly where two colors meet. For embellishment, use tiny grains and seeds from your spice rack, setting them into the sand with tweezers if necessary.

After the glue has dried, remove excess sand by lightly brushing it away. Or turn the painting upside down and shake it gently, or run a vacuum cleaner a few inches above the surface. If you try to remove unwanted sand before the glue is dry, the colors may spread into each other. Any mistake can be scraped away when the glue is dry and corrected with more glue and sand.

Paint and Color
A sand-layered planter

Traditional sand painting is done in two dimensions, but working in the round, with sand layering, is more popular today. Among the favorite projects are decorative arrangements in see-through flowerpots and terrariums. Detailed instructions for making the flowerpot shown at right are on the pages that follow. With practice, you could make a panoramic landscape terrarium like the one shown at the bottom of the page. You will need a clear glass container. Any empty jar or bottle with a wide neck is suitable, as long as there are no distracting markings. In addition to

You can give a cactus a desert home by pouring and spooning a southwest landscape into an old food jar or other transparent container. Mountains, greenery, and birds in flight are easy designs to make.

The dancing girl departs from the usual horizontal layering of sand. To forestall a cave-in, she was built up in stages, as the blue background on either side was filled in for support.

Motifs for cactus plantings that require little skill to execute include (left to right): a silhouette of a pet, a stylized view of blossoms, and a brilliantly colored woodland duck.

Sand layering is effective when it is done in the round as a continuous panorama, especially if you can display the finished work so it can be viewed from all sides. The photographs below show four sides of a square terrarium. In the actual glass cube, the far left and far right edges meet like the intermediate ones, so the scene is continuous.

2: To start sand layering, pour or spoon a thin base layer of sand into the container to represent the extreme foreground of your picture. Avoid a too-even look.

3: To make jagged clumps of grass, use a pointed tool to force sand at intervals from a top layer down into a layer of green sand just below. Be careful not to go beyond the green layer.

4: A spoonful of sand poured against the glass becomes a mountain. Ring the container with a chain of mountains, linking them base to base. Keep filling in the center to forestall a cave-in.

the pouring spoon described previously, you will need a regular spoon and a sharpened ¼-inch dowel or other pointed tool. Work on a stable surface. If you need to lift the container, keep it level. When you buy sand for a planter, be sure it is colorfast to avoid color washouts.

Contours in Sand

The easiest theme for beginners is a mountain scene; making it is almost as simple as dropping sand from a spoon. The foreground is made first, since near objects appear low in the composition. Farther objects, and eventually the sky, are layered over them. To start, pour a layer of purple or beige sand onto the bottom of the jar (photograph 2). The layer should be quite thin. If your jar is, for example, 4 inches tall and 3 inches wide, make this and each of the succeeding base layers roughly ¼ inch deep. You needn't be meticulous at this point; a few casual spoonfuls of sand work well, since gentle swells and hollows make the terrain image more realistic.

Only sand that shows through the sides of the container figures in the finished work. With large containers, you may want to conserve colored sand by using plain soil, coarse sand, or gravel in the center—or salvage colored sand that has gotten mixed together. It is possible to fill the center with plastic foam, but I find this awkward.

Over the bottom layer of sand, pour a second layer. Choose a color that will blend, such as pale green or pink. Continue adding colors in varying depths—some in unbroken layers, others in spotty patches to avoid a too-neat, striped design.

Grass

After four or five layers are in place, put some vegetation in your picture by pouring a layer of dark-green sand, followed by a layer of another color, perhaps orange. With the pointed stick held against the side of the container, lightly pierce the orange layer, continuing to the bottom of the green layer (photograph 3). Grains of orange sand will filter down into the green belt in a ragged pattern, simulating tufts of grass. If you rotate the container with your free hand as you alternately lower and withdraw the stick, you can produce a wavy line.

When you are satisfied with the foreground—from six to twelve layers is suggested—you are ready to build the mountain range.

Mountains

With an unbent spoon, take up sand of a color appropriate to mountains—perhaps brown, blue, or purple—and gently pour it against the side of your container (photograph 4). This will produce a round-topped mountain. If you would like a sharper peak, raise the spoon as you pour. Pour the rest of the mountains around the container in similar fashion, just far enough apart so their bases join. You can make a second range of mountains by pouring sand of a lighter shade but the same color between the mountains of the first chain. If you want snow-capped peaks in

5: To make a bird on the wing, start by pouring a thin spot of white sand against the glass in the blue of the sky. Use the tip of the bent spoon for pinpoint control.

6: With a pointed stick, depress the middle of the white spot so a few grains of white sand are pushed slightly downward, thus forming the bird's head and wings.

7: Without delay, gently cover the completed bird with additional blue sky sand so its fragile outline is frozen in place. Repeat this technique with each subsequent bird.

the second range, flatten the tops with a sidewise movement of the pointed stick; then place a spoonful of white sand on each little platform you have made. Use the bent spoon for this; it will deposit sand in a smaller area than the open spoon. Using the pointed stick, jab this white sand into the top of the mountain at intervals to represent snow. Above the jagged area, pour additional white sand to give the mountain a sharp peak.

Throughout this mountain-building process, keep filling in the center of the container as you build up the picture on the outside. Otherwise the sand will tend to slide away from the glass.

It is easy to place a rising (or setting) sun between two mountains. Pour a spoonful of yellow sand as though you were making a small mountain. If you move the spoon gently back and forth as you pour, you can make a rounded half-sun; adjust the sand with the tip of the spoon if necessary. Cover the sun and mountains with a layer of blue sand to hold them in place and to represent the lower part of the sky.

Birds

The easiest creatures to introduce into sand layering are birds in flight. You can depict them head-on by pouring a short, thin spot of white sand on the sky layer (photograph 5), then forcing a few grains down into the blue sand below (photograph 6). When the pointed stick is withdrawn, the bird's head and wings will be formed. Place more blue sand over the white sand to hold the bird in place (photograph 7). Repeat at other points, remembering that progressively smaller birds will seem to recede into the distance.

Clouds

At this point, you could finish the sky with blue sand, or you could add a few clouds, as pictured in the panoramic terrarium on page 1891. To make clouds, pour a thicker spot of white sand and pierce it at several points. You can round the ends of the clouds, whittling back unwanted white sand with the stick as you replace the white sand by pouring in blue sand. You can make the clouds seem to recede into the distance by making them progressively smaller. Complete the sky with a solid layer of blue. Keep about one-third of the container empty for planting.

Planting

The most congenial and appropriate plant to use in a sand-layered container is a cactus. Cacti grow naturally in arid regions in soil that is largely sand. So fill the top of the container with a mixture that is half potting soil and half sand. Cacti are shallow-rooted. With the blunt end of a dowel, make a small hole in the mixture and plant the cactus in it.

You can create a miniature desert landscape around the cactus if you like. Bits of tree bark, for example, look like desert rock formations. Small rocks can look like mountains. But a handful of white gravel will serve just as well as a finishing touch.

Do not use bright aquarium gravel that would compete with the bold colors of the layered sand below.

With a richer soil—peat moss or humus in place of sand in the planting mixture—you can grow ferns in this container. Better still, use a covered container with a good amount of space on top of the sand layering (such as an apothecary jar) so you can install a terrarium. Place a layer of gravel atop your painting, a bit of powdered charcoal on top of the gravel to keep the soil sweet, and a rich soil mixture above this. Then grow a garden of miniatures within this microenvironment.

Paint and Color
An illusionary fishbowl

Simulating an underwater scene such as the one shown opposite will give you a chance to blend sand layers of luminous greens and blues, while depicting aquatic creatures real or fantastic. You can use any transparent container, but a fishbowl is a natural setting for a sand painting of marine life.

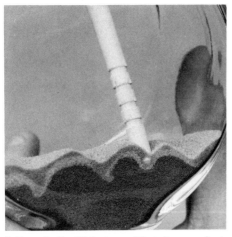

8: To make the thick stems of the tall, wavy plants in the aquatic scene, pour several layers of blue and green sand over the bottom layers. With a blunt stick, press these top layers into the lower one at intervals.

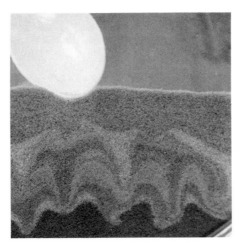

9: To make a hollow for the body of a fish, press the tip of the spoon into the blue sand.

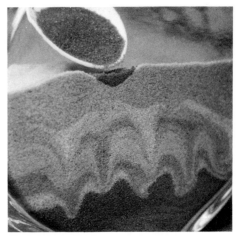

10: Fill the hollow with sand of a bright color. Reds, oranges, and yellows stand out.

Making Contours

Pour a layer of beige sand on the bottom of the container, following the instructions on page 1892. This will be the ocean floor in your painting. The more the layers undulate, the better. Next pour a thin layer of dark green sand and above that a layer of lighter green. With a sharp stick held against the glass, pierce through the two layers of green and into the beige sand below. This will make lines that will represent low aquatic plants. Cover these with a zone of dark blue water, while filling the center of the bowl to avoid cave-ins.

At this point, you can add more elaborate plants by using pink and red sand. Pour a short, thick mound on top of the blue sand. Then, using the blunt end of the stick this time, push down hard into the blue sand to about twice the depth of the top mound (photograph 8). This will start a thick stem. Remove the stick, and on top of the stem, drip a horizontal layer of sand from a spoon. This will be the first branch. Add more blue sand. Repeat this on either side of the stem as many times as you like, building up a new layer of background color as you complete each branch, and prolonging the stem as you made the first stem. If you like, you can put short stems at the ends of branches to give them a twisted effect. The sand may put more ripple into your lines than you intend, but you can blame it on water distortion.

Fish

To start the body of a fish, press the tip of a spoon into the sand (photograph 9). Since most fish are not round, make the depression in the sand much the shape of the spoon itself. Fill the hollow (photograph 10) with any color that pleases you; tropical fish exist in almost any conceivable hue. Instead of just one color, you

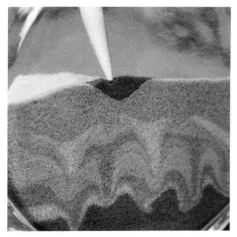

11: For an eye, make a tiny depression with a pointed stick near one end of the body.

12: Fill in the eye with a few grains of black sand, using the bent spoon for pinpoint control.

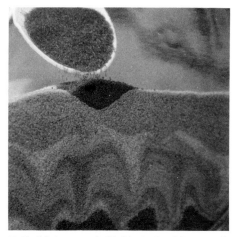

13: Build the upper half of the body with a mound of sand until it is the same shape as the lower half.

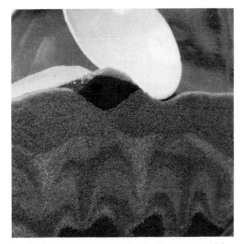

14: Make a second hollow for the lower part of the tail, about half as wide and deep as the first one.

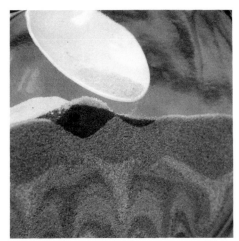

15: For an exotic look, fill the tail hollow with thin layers of sand of various colors.

This eye-fooling fishbowl needs no help from plants to make its point. Although sand layering owes much of its popularity to terrarium enthusiasts, you can enjoy it with or without a green thumb.

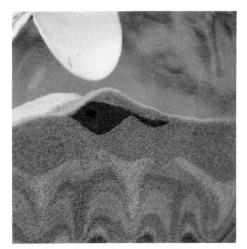

16: Cover the body and the lower half of the tail with a thin layer of the blue sand (water).

17: To make the upper half of the tail, first spoon a thin band of matching sand above the lower half.

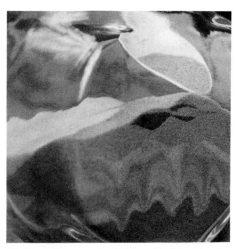

18: Cover the upper half of the tail with more of the background color, blue, to hold it in place.

might pour alternating layers within the hollow—thin strips of white between bands of another color to get an iridescent gleam. Give the fish an eye (photographs 11 and 12, page 1895). Match the shape of the hollow with a mound of sand above it to produce a symmetrical body (photograph 13, page 1895).

For the tail, press the spoon into the sand to make a depression at the rear of the fish at a slight angle to the body (photograph 14, page 1895). Fill this trough level (photograph 15, page 1895).

Blending colors in the tail will give you a filmy, underwater look. For example, if the body of the fish is red, you might make the first layer of the tail red, the next orange, and the last yellow. Or you could make the tail a single hue. This completes the lower half of the tail. Top it with a thin layer of the sand color you have been using for water (photograph 16). Upon this, place a small, sloping hill of the same color or colors used in the lower half of the tail, making a mirror image of it (photograph 17). Now cover the entire fish with blue sand (photograph 18).

Make other fish of various colors and sizes at different levels of the fishbowl. Experiment with different shapes. You can make a swordfish, for example, by extending a flat layer of sand out from the head just before you start the upper half.

Complete the underwater scene by filling the container with blue sand, gradually using lighter shades as you near the surface. Color tones can be blended by stirring them lightly with the point of a stick.

Paint and Color
A fantasy garden

Once you have mastered the basics of sand layering, you may want to try an impressionistic garden scene bursting with color (as shown opposite). Assemble an array of vivid hues, and create some of your own by mixing sand colors just as you would oil paints. If the sand is fine, grains in the mixture will be almost imperceptible. If you are using a coarse grade of sand, you will get an interesting grainy look.

Begin your scene with several layers of green, using different shades. Make hillocks of grass by pouring a layer of greenish-yellow sand over the top green layer and pushing it into the lower layers at intervals. Place bright blobs of color on the tallest green tufts of grass (photograph 19). This will give you a flower border to build on. Be careful with color rather than detail here, since these flowers will be too small for intricacy. Anchor these blossoms by pressing down through them with the pointed stick into the top of a grass tuft. This will provide a stem for the flowers, and keep them from collapsing. So will additional yellow-green sand that you place on either side of the flowers, and filler sand that you place in the center of the container. If you like, you can add another row of flowers by using a layer of plain yellow to set them off.

19: To start the garden scene, use a bent spoon to fill depressions in the grassy foreground layers with bright, flowery patches of color.

A sun that is rising or setting is easy to add to a sand-layered scene. A mountain of yellow sand is turned into a half-sun by maneuvering background sand in at the base.

A fanciful garden scene includes petaled flowers, a fierce-looking bumblebee in intricate detail, and banks of clouds in a deep blue sky, all above a foreground of a grassy, flowered meadow.

20: With a blunt stick, push green sand down into the ground layer to make the stems of tall flowers.

21: The first rose petal is formed by pouring a shallow red mound to one side on a green stem.

22: Outline and highlight the flower petal with a thin covering of pink or white sand.

23: Build a second petal upon the first one, and continue in this way until your rose takes shape.

24: To make a tulip of sand, pour a single mound of color atop the stem hollow and cover it with sky.

25: Then, with a pointed stick, poke deep grooves from the sky layer into the top of the tulip.

Garden Beauties

Above this low border grow whatever tall garden flowers you would like to make. These long-stemmed flowers may be set against a background of intense blue. Choose this color carefully. Begin by building a layer of sky about ½ inch deep. Then make tall stems by placing a thick, short mound of green sand on top of this, one for each stem. With the blunt end of the stick, poke each of these mounds down to the ground level (photograph 20). Fill in with more green sand if necessary to get a fairly thick stem. On each side of the top of the stem, place a low mound of the same green sand to represent leaves. If you like, outline the tops of the leaves with yellow-green. Add more blue as needed to support the mounds. To create a rose petal, place a shallow mound of red or pink sand on the stem (photograph 21). With the stick, push the red or pink sand firmly up at the sides while coaxing the blue sand sky inward and upward beneath the red. Edge the petal in pink or white (photograph 22), and place another above the first and slightly to one side of it (photograph 23). After some practice, you will be able to make tightly petaled, graceful buds. If the petals are floppy, you are not pushing the sand up firmly enough with the pointed stick. A tulip is made by placing a mound of color on a flower stem (photograph 24) and poking fringes into the top with the pointed stick (photograph 25). Grains of yellow sand atop the centers of each tulip will suggest pistils.

Fill the sky above your garden with a variety of birds. Make them in two or three colors instead of one, and vary the wingspans and body forms. For example, if you push extra sand into the body as with the pointed stick, the bird will be plumper.

26: Prepare to make a bee by forming a small hollow with the tip of the bent spoon.

27: Fill the hollow with yellow sand, and poke two antennae down into the blue underlayer.

28: For the bee's eyes, pour dark sand into two tiny depressions in the head.

29: Round out the head with layers of yellow and black sand.

30: Extend wings on either side of the bee's head with long, thin layers of orange or white sand.

31: Pour clouds in layers of pink and white. Scallop the bottoms with a pointed stick.

Insects

You may want to make some insects too. To make a fat bumblebee like the one pictured, begin with the head. Place a tiny hollow in the sky sand (photograph 26), and fill it with yellow sand. Extend antennae downward from the head to make a bee that seems tilted forward by forcing a bit of head sand down into the blue layer beneath (photograph 27). Poke two tiny dots for the eyes at the top of the yellow semicircle and fill these with black sand (photograph 28). Complete the head by spooning semicircles of yellow and black sand onto and around the eyes (photograph 29). Next place a wide arc of orange or white sand on either side of the bee's head (photograph 30). The white will approximate the rapidly moving wings of a bee in flight; if you prefer, orange suggests a gliding flight pattern. With such delicate work, you must keep building up the central core or these creatures will collapse. Finish building the rest of the bee's body with thin alternating layers of black and yellow sand of about the same width as those used for the head. Finally cover and stabilize the bee with a layer of blue sky. Other insects are just as easy to make. Whether you use long layers to make dragonflies or tiny dabs to make mosquitoes, the basic technique is the same.

When your garden is comfortably filled with flowers, birds, and bees, check the remaining space in the container. If space permits, add a cloud or two, the bottoms scalloped with a bit of color to heighten the fantasy (photograph 31). Don't wedge the clouds too tightly; they should seem to float in the sky.

For related crafts and projects, see "Stone Painting," "Terrariums," and "Vegetable Dyes."

SASHIMI AND SUSHI
Raw Fish, Vinegared Rice

Imagine sinking your teeth into a morsel of food that resembles, in taste and texture, the finest rare beef. Imagine this food to be delicately and perfectly seasoned, artfully served, so tender it can easily be severed with a chopstick. Then imagine your surprise when you discover that you are eating one of the great delicacies of Japan—raw fish. Sashimi (fresh, uncooked fish) and sushi (various rice dishes in which raw fish is a recurring ingredient) may seem less than appetizing to the uninitiated, even those who consume raw clams and oysters with gusto. But as is the case with many exotic foods, once the crisis of the first sampling is over, many non-Japanese consider sashimi and sushi to be two of the gastronomic wonders of the world. Uncooked fish—and only absolutely fresh fillets of salt-water species are recommended for these dishes—neither tastes nor smells the way you might expect. It has no fishy odor and no fishy taste. Anyone who has tasted tuna sushi, for example, will find it impossible to believe it is even remotely related to the familiar canned variety. (For those who would still prefer to eat only cooked fish, there are two types of sushi—*chirashi sushi*, page 1911; and *norimaki sushi*, page 1908—that can be prepared without raw fish.)

How to Serve Sashimi and Sushi

Sashimi and sushi are not made by plunking a whole or even a part of a raw fish on a plate. They consist of bite-sized chunks or slivers of boneless, skinless fillets of such fish as sea bass, striped bass, tuna, red snapper, and salmon. Like other Japanese dishes, sashimi and sushi are prepared and served elegantly and delicately, with the color, shape, and texture of the main ingredients, garnishes, and containers harmoniously balanced. Either dish may be composed of a variety of kinds of fish. Except for *chirashi sushi*—which is always served in individual bowls—the fillets are arranged attractively either on individual plates or on a large platter from which each guest makes a selection to transfer to his own plate. Each morsel is then picked up with chopsticks and dipped into a sauce just before it is eaten. A charming preliminary to any Japanese meal is the *oshibori*, a tightly rolled hand towel that has been dampened with very hot water, occasionally scented. Each guest receives his own *oshibori*, on a small tray, with which to wipe his hands (and face, if he wishes).

In Japan, sushi and sashimi are often eaten at a *sushiya*, a restaurant that specializes in these dishes. *Sushiyas* are typically sparkling clean, small, and cheery, with a relaxed, informal atmosphere similar to that of an English pub. The customer has the choice of being served at a table in a booth, or at the sushi counter near the front of the restaurant. A true enthusiast sits on a stool at the sushi counter and orders his favorite types, a pair at a time, selected from the refrigerated glass case behind the counter. In about half a minute, the cook cuts the fish, forms rice into balls, and places before the customer a perfect pair of sushi of the type requested.

Sashimi is usually thought of as an appetizer; the meal is rounded out with sake or beer, green tea, sushi or another Japanese dish, and soup. Fresh fruit is the usual dessert in Japan. You may choose to structure a meal the same way, or to serve sashimi and sushi both as appetizers, or to offer them as hors d'oeuvres. Add the suggested garnishes, edible and inedible, to your carefully arranged plates of fish, and use as many Japanese ingredients as you can. Even if it seems impossible to duplicate the atmosphere of a *sushiya* or a Japanese home, you can savor many varieties of these Japanese specialties.

Sushi, a Japanese dish made with sweetened, vinegared rice and bite-sized pieces of fish (usually raw, but sometimes cooked or marinated), vegetables, and cooked egg forms the basis of the meal pictured opposite and keyed at right. Soy sauce (for dipping) and green tea complete the meal. The tightly rolled hand towel is dampened with very hot water and is used before meals to freshen the face and hands. Sushi is usually eaten with chopsticks, but it may also be picked up with the fingers.

Kozo Wada was born in Japan and is one of three cooks behind the sushi bar at Yamashiro, a Japanese restaurant in New York. In addition to making superb sashimi and sushi as fast as the eye can follow, Mr. Wada is famous for his unique hairdo and the hachimaki, *or wrapped scarf, he wears while working.*

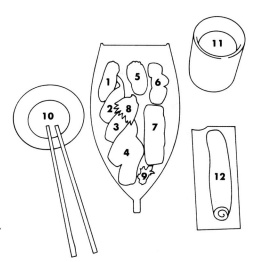

In the boat-shaped dish are (1) raw striped bass; (2) cooked shrimp; (3) marinated sardine; (4) raw tuna; (5) salmon roe (red caviar) wrapped in dried seaweed (*nori*); (6) rolls of rice filled with cucumber and wrapped in *nori*; (7) a piece of egg omelette flavored with soy sauce, rice wine, and sugar; (8) cucumber sliced into a decorative fan shape; and (9) slices of pickled ginger to be eaten between the different flavors to refresh the palate. Accompanying the dish of sushi are (10) a saucer of soy sauce; (11) green tea; and (12) a hand towel (*oshibori*).

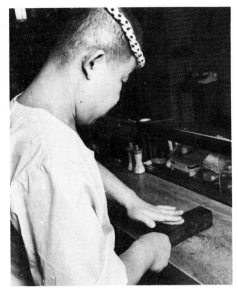

To prepare sashimi and sushi, you must cut and slice raw fish in special ways. Your success will depend on the sharpness of your knife and the skill with which you use that knife. Above, Kozo Wada is pictured sharpening his *yanagi* knife on a *toischi* stone, a ritual he performs once a day. In the old days, the sashimi master sharpened his knife 24 hours before he used it, keeping the blade immersed in water during this interval so the smell of the whetted blade would not contaminate the fish on the day it was served.

Special ingredients for sashimi and sushi

Daikon: Japanese white radish, a great deal larger than the American variety; lettuce or icicle radish may be substituted.
Dashi: basic soup and cooking stock; instant dashi is available in packages.
Ginger: pickled ginger comes ready-to-use in jars.
Kanpyo: dried gourd shavings; available packaged.
Mirin: sweet Japanese rice wine used as a seasoning; dry sherry and sugar may be substituted.
Nori: dried seaweed available in thin greenish-black 7-by-7-inch sheets.
Sake: Japanese rice wine; dry white wine or dry sherry may be substituted.
Shoyu: soy sauce made from soy beans, barley or wheat, salt, water, and rice enzymes; Japanese soy sauce, more delicate and less salty than Chinese soy sauce, is a basic ingredient in Japanese cuisine.
Su: rice vinegar; distilled cider vinegar may be substituted.
Wasabi: Japanese horseradish, often called Japanese mustard; it comes in powder form, and must be mixed with hot water to form a paste for sashimi and sushi. Yellow dry mustard may be substituted.

To make sashimi and sushi, Kozo Wada uses these Japanese utensils (you may substitute Western utensils). From top to bottom are: a *yanagi*, a knife for cutting fish for sushi; a *deba-bocho* or general fish-cutting knife; a pair of metal-tipped chopsticks for picking up and arranging food; and a *sudare*, the bamboo mat used for rolling *norimaki sushi*.

Ingredients

The raw fish used for sashimi and sushi must be absolutely fresh. When you buy the fish, make sure that the flesh is firm, the skin is not slimy, the eyes are bright and clear, and that there is no old fishy odor. Do not use frozen fish. Avoid fresh-water fish from rivers or lakes that might be polluted.

To bring out the special taste of these Japanese foods, try to use authentic Japanese ingredients. These unique ingredients and possible substitutions are explained in the ingredients glossary (left). If there is no substitution listed and the original ingredient is unavailable, it is better to leave it out entirely than to try a substitution of your own.

Utensils

Japanese kitchen utensils used to prepare sashimi and sushi are pictured above, but Western utensils make perfectly good substitutes. Because cutting and slicing play such a large role in the preparation of these dishes, work on a large cutting board or butcher-block counter, and use a sharp, heavy kitchen knife for cutting. A flexible bamboo table mat or a clean terry cloth hand towel may be substituted for the *sudare* used in rolling up *norimaki sushi* (page 1908). Various cooking operations will require standard items such as large and small saucepans, a small skillet, and a large nonmetallic bowl.

Where to Buy Japanese Ingredients and Utensils

The Japanese ingredients and utensils used in the recipes given here can be purchased at food shops in oriental neighborhoods and in the gourmet sections of some large supermarkets and department stores. If needed ingredients are unavailable in your area, write to one of the regional offices of the Japan Food Corporation for the name of the retail store nearest you.

Addresses of Japan Food Corporation offices are:
Baltimore area: 92-25 Berger Road, Columbia, Md. 21046.
Chicago: 1850 West 43rd Street, Chicago, Ill. 60609
Houston: 3305 Sulrose Street, Houston, Texas 77006.
Los Angeles: 1131 Mateo Street, Los Angeles, Calif. 90021
New York: 11-31 31st Avenue, Long Island City, New York 11106.
Sacramento: 1515 North C Street, Sacramento, Calif. 95814.
San Francisco: 445 Kauffman Court, South San Francisco, Calif. 94080.
Toronto: 25-6 Connel Court, Toronto, Ontario, Canada.

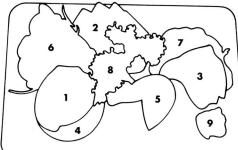

Many garnishes can be used to decorate a plate of sashimi (slices of uncooked fish). Shown above and keyed at left are: (1) a rosette made from slices of fluke with a center of red caviar; (2) tuna; (3) striped bass; garnished with (4 and 5) lemon slices (to be squeezed over the striped bass); (6 and 7) mounds of shredded *daikon* (Japanese radish); (8) parsley; and (9) a ball of *wasabi* paste; (green mustard to be mixed with soy sauce to make a dipping sauce). Other garnishes that might have been used include seasonal flowers, tiny (inedible) orchids, or small flowers sculpted from cucumber slices.

Kitchen Favorites and Celebrations
Sashimi

$ ⊠ ♠ 🏺

Sashimi, although simple to prepare, requires skill in cutting the fish and in arranging slices and garnishes on the serving plate. Many fish are suitable, although some are more highly prized than others. Try some or all of those listed below to find out which you prefer. Each fish has a distinct flavor, and the textures vary from the tenderness of tuna, which almost melts in your mouth, to the resilience of abalone, which provides an exercise in chewing patience. When you serve sashimi, allow about four ounces of fish per person.

Ingredients

Raw seafood such as tuna, sea bream, fluke, trout, striped bass, sea bass, halibut, mackerel, red snapper, octopus, squid, abalone, scallops, or cuttlefish

Daikon (Japanese radish)
Wasabi paste (Japanese mustard)
Soy sauce for dipping
Lemon slices, sliced pickled ginger, and parsley for garnish

Clean the seafood, removing the bones and skin. Use only the best parts for sashimi. Clean and fillet the fish yourself (right) or have the fishmonger do it for you. Put the fillets in a colander and pour boiling water over them; then immediately immerse them in cold water. (The boiling water is used to destroy any surface bacteria, not to cook the fish.) Keep the sashimi cool, and prepare it quickly to preserve its freshness.

CRAFTNOTES: HOW TO FILLET A FISH

Scale and wash the whole fish in cold water. To scale it, lay the fish on your cutting surface, and grasp the head firmly with one hand. Hold the knife almost vertically, and scrape off all the scales, working from the tail to the head.

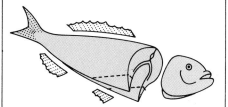

Cut off the fins, head, and hard flaps near the head (dotted lines above). Then gut the fish by slitting the entire length of the belly and removing the entrails.

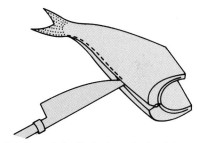

Cut through the flesh along the back from the head to the tail (dotted line above).

Turn the knife flat and cut the fish laterally above the backbone from head to tail. The knife will run along the rib bones, and the fillet will lift off in one piece (above). Turn the fish over and repeat on the other side.

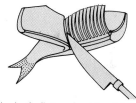

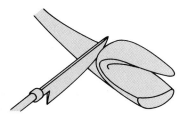

To skin the fillets, lay them skin-side down and grasp the tail end with one hand. Insert the knife at the tail; cut and push the flesh away with the side of the blade (above).

1: Crosscut the fish fillet at a slight angle, using a single stroke for each ¼-inch-thick slice. The pieces should be no more than 1½ inches across.

2: Some fish, such as the tuna shown here, are tender enough so they can be cut slightly thicker than ¼ inch. Tuna may also be cut into cubes.

3: To begin forming a fish rosette, arrange three slices of fish on the cutting surface. Start at the right and overlap the ends ½ to 1 inch.

Preparing Sashimi

SLICING THE FISH: Make sure your cutting board and knife are clean and wet. Large fish fillets will first need to be cut in half lengthwise. Then slice them into bite-sized pieces (photograph 1). Some kinds of fish, such as tuna, may be sliced slightly thicker (photograph 2). Tuna, because it is firm, can also be cut into ½-inch cubes. Other fish, such as striped bass, are occasionally sliced so thin the slices appear transparent when they are arranged on a plate. You may want to try your hand at forming rosettes from large, thin slices (photographs 3 to 6 show fluke being shaped this way). Scallops, because they are small, may be left uncut.

PREPARING GARNISHES: In Japan, various garnishes are used, some edible, some merely beautiful. Your garden will furnish inedible as well as edible garnishes, since flowers and sprigs of delicate greenery are often part of a sashimi platter. To prepare *daikon,* (an edible Japanese white radish) as a garnish, shred it finely with a knife or grate it, using the coarse blade of a grater. If *daikon* is unavailable, you may use finely shredded lettuce. *Wasabi,* a Japanese horseradish, is used to enhance the flavor of the fish and as an aid to digestion. The *wasabi* comes in powder form (dry yellow mustard may be substituted); mix *wasabi* with a little water to make a thick paste and form the paste into a ball with your fingers. Cut lemon into thin slices; they will be squeezed over portions of white fish.

Serving Sashimi

Sashimi may be served on individual plates or on one large platter from which each diner makes a selection. The fish may be placed on a bed of shredded *daikon,* or

4: Using chopsticks or another suitable utensil, begin rolling the slices into a cone shape. Use the fingers of the other hand as a guide.

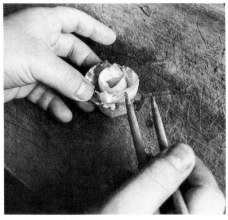

5: Arrange the petals with the tip of the chopsticks to form the rosette shape. If the flower falls apart, you need to overlap the slices more.

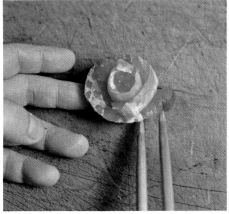

6: To complete the rosette, put a bit of red caviar (salmon roe) at the center. If caviar is not available, substitute a tiny sprig of parsley.

placed between two mounds of it. For each person, form a ball from one teaspoon of *wasabi* paste and place it on the plate. Give each person a small, shallow bowl containing soy sauce. Each guest mixes as much of the *wasabi* as he desires into his soy sauce. He then picks up the fish with chopsticks and dips it into the sauce before eating it. The other garnishes may be arranged as you wish.

Kitchen Favorites and Celebrations
Nigiri sushi

This is the easiest type of sushi to prepare. The rice is cooked and mixed with a sweetened vinegar solution ahead of time. The cooled rice is then formed into small oblongs and topped with bite-sized pieces of raw seafood, cooked seafood, or egg which has been made into a thick omelette. Because of the variety of toppings available and the volume in which the dish is consumed, *nigiri sushi* is often called the sandwich of Japan.

Ingredients
Sushi rice (recipe at right; 3 cups of cooked rice will make about 4 dozen *nigiri sushi*

Raw fish (page 1903) and other toppings, such as raw clams, salmon roe, sea urchin, shrimp (boiled), eel (cooked), sardines (marinated), or eggs (a thick omelette; recipe page 1906)

Wasabi (Japanese mustard)
Pickled ginger
Soy sauce
Nori (dried seaweed)
Salt
Su (rice vinegar)
Sugar
Lemon
Sake

Sushi rice
Rice cooked for sushi is slightly firmer than rice for other dishes. This recipe yields about 6 cups of cooked rice.

Ingredients
2 cups raw Japanese or unconverted white rice
2½ cups water
¼ cup **su** (rice vinegar)
2 tablespoons sugar
2 teaspoons salt
1½ tablespoons **mirin** (sweet rice wine)
Wash the rice thoroughly; let drain and stand for one hour before cooking. Put the rice and water into a heavy-bottomed saucepan and bring to a boil. Cover saucepan, and simmer for 15 to 20 minutes, until the rice is just tender. Remove from heat and let stand, covered, for 10 minutes. Put the vinegar, sugar, salt and **mirin** into a small saucepan and bring to a boil. Remove from heat. Put the hot rice in a large nonmetallic bowl. Pour the vinegar solution over the rice, mixing it in with quick strokes. Fan the rice while you are mixing—this cools the rice quickly and produces a glossy sheen that is desirable in a good sushi base. The rice is ready when it cools to room temperature. It may be stored in a cool place up to five hours. Do not refrigerate it as this will harden it.

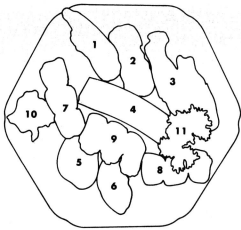

The five pieces on the top half of the plate are *nigiri sushi;* topping the mounds of rice are (1) marinated sardine; (2) raw tuna; (3) raw striped bass; and (4) egg cooked into an omelette. The two pieces at the bottom of the plate are (5) sea urchin and (6) salmon roe (variations of *nigiri sushi*). The curved row of *norimaki sushi* is comprised of (7 and 8) raw tuna and (9) cucumber fillings. Garnishing the dish are (10) sliced pickled ginger and (11) a sprig of parsley.

Nigiri sushi (small mounds of vinegared rice with various toppings) and *norimaki sushi* (rolls of vinegared rice with various fillings wrapped in seaweed) are pictured above and keyed at right. These two types of sushi are often served together.

7: To make *nigiri sushi*, start by slicing sashimi (the raw fish) into 1-by-2-inch pieces ¼ inch thick. Cut at the angle shown.

8: Place the piece of fish in the palm of one hand. Pick up a bit of *wasabi* paste on the index finger of the other hand, and spread it on the fish.

9: In your free hand, form about 1 tablespoon of the sushi rice into an oblong, and place it on the *wasabi* side of the fish.

Sushi egg omelette
Ingredients
3 eggs
1 tablespoon sugar
1 teaspoon soy sauce
¼ teaspoon salt
1½ tablespoons **mirin** (sweet rice wine)
2 tablespoons **dashi** (soup stock) or water
Vegetable oil
Place all the ingredients in a bowl and beat together well. Pour the mixture into a heated skillet, preferably a small square one, that has been brushed with vegetable oil. Cover, and cook the omelette over a low flame until it is set. It should be 1/3- to 1/2-inch thick.

Basic Nigiri Sushi With Raw Fish

How to make the most common type of *nigiri sushi*, using raw fish, is demonstrated in photographs 7 to 11. Cook the rice ahead of time so it can cool thoroughly. Clean and fillet the fish as described on page 1903. Have a small bowl of *wasabi* paste handy to spread on the underside of the sashimi slices (*wasabi* comes in powder form; mix it with a little water to form the paste). And keep a bowl of water within reach so you can moisten your hands frequently (while forming the oblongs) to keep the rice from sticking to them. When you have mastered the technique pictured, try the other toppings that follow.

Other Toppings

SHRIMP: Shrimp are eaten raw in Japan, but unless you purchase them live and are sure they were taken from pure waters, cook them in boiling water until they turn pink. Before cooking, cut off the heads of the shrimp and spear each one with a toothpick (photograph 12). After the shrimp has been cooked, withdraw the toothpick, peel off the shell, and devein the shrimp with the point of a knife. Then split the shrimp (photograph 13), open it up, spread on *wasabi*, and place on top of the rice oblong.

EGG: Make the omelette recipe (left). Let it cool; then cut it into 1-by-3-inch rectangles. With a knife, cut a ½-by-3½-inch strip of *nori*—the dried seaweed—for each egg rectangle. Omit the *wasabi* paste and place the egg on top of the rice oblong; wrap the *nori* strip around both (photograph 14), using a few grains of rice between the overlapping edges of *nori* to hold them together.

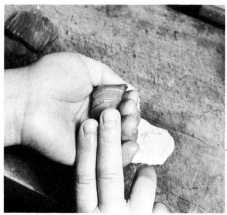

10: In order to make the fish adhere to the rice, smooth down the sides of the slice over the rice, using thumb and forefinger.

11: Then press down on the top so the fish and the rice, prepared as described on page 1905, remain stuck together.

12: To prevent the shrimp from curling up while they are cooking, insert a toothpick in each one from front to back.

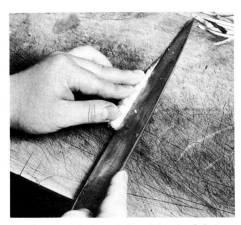

13: Slit the cooked, peeled, and deveined shrimp along the inside curve. Then open it out and flatten it, butterfly fashion.

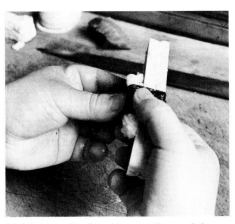

14: Wrap a strip of *nori* (seaweed) around the rectangle of egg omelette and the oblong of rice to hold them together.

15: Place the eel on top of the rice oblong. Over the eel, brush a sauce made by adding a bit of sugar and sake (rice wine) to a base of soy sauce.

EEL: Boil the eel one and one half to two hours in a solution of 10 parts water, 1 part sugar, 1 part sake, and 1 part soy sauce. Let the eel cool; then clean it and cut it into bite-sized pieces about the same size as the rice oblongs (photograph 15).

SARDINES: Marinate the sardines for two hours in a solution of 10 tablespoons rice vinegar, 1 tablespoon salt, and 1 tablespoon sugar. Split the marinated sardines in half and place each half on top of the rice. The sardine may be seasoned with *wasabi* or grated fresh ginger. If you wish, add a decorative touch by making cuts in the surface of the sardine (photograph 16).

CLAMS: Place a clam (whole or sliced, depending on its size) on top of an oblong of rice and sprinkle it with lemon juice.

SALMON ROE or SEA URCHIN: Because of the fluid consistency of these two foods, circle the rice with a retaining wall of *nori* to form a special type of *nigiri sushi*. Cut a strip of *nori* measuring about 1 by 6 inches. Form the oblong of rice, and wrap the *nori* strip around it (photograph 17); hold the overlapping ends together by using a few grains of rice as glue. Pile the roe or sea urchin on top of the rice (photograph 18), and sprinkle with lemon juice. Scallops, chopped into small pieces, are also occasionally prepared and served this way.

Serving

Nigiri sushi is often served along with *norimaki sushi* (rolls of sushi rice wrapped in sheets of seaweed with various fillings, page 1908) and garnished with lemon slices and pickled ginger. The pieces are picked up with chopsticks or fingers, then dipped into soy sauce before eating.

16: Sardines may be decorated by making shallow cuts in the top surface. Use a sharp knife, and have the fish on a towel to soften the cuts.

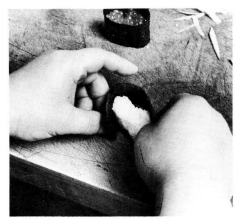

17: When a retaining wall is needed for a soft topping, make the rice oblong a bit shorter than usual, and wrap a strip of *nori* around it.

18: Pick up about a teaspoon of salmon roe or sea urchin, and put it on top of the rice; the topping should come up to the edge of the *nori*.

1907

19: To make tuna rolls, moisten hands and fingers; then spread about ¼ cup of sushi rice over the *nori* (dried seaweed), leaving 1 inch at the top and bottom uncovered.

20: Put on a strip of *wasabi* paste and cover it with a layer of tuna sushi, cut into small pieces.

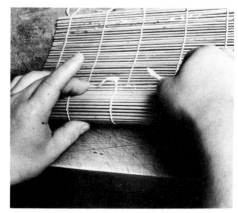

21: Use the bamboo mat (or a hand towel) to help you roll the *nori* and its contents into a cylinder.

Futomaki sushi is a special type of *norimaki sushi*. Large cylinders of rice are stuffed with egg omelette, sliced cucumber, dried mushrooms, dried gourd shavings, and cod roe. The cylinder is wrapped with dried seaweed and sliced for serving, as pictured.

Kitchen Favorites and Celebrations
Norimaki sushi $ ▮ ⚦ ⚱

Norimaki means rolled in seaweed, and this type of sushi, pictured above and on pages 1900 and 1905, resembles a jelly roll. The rice is rolled into cylinders with an outer sheath of seaweed and an inner core of fish, egg, mushrooms, and other ingredients. The bamboo mat pictured, called a *sudare*, is used to facilitate rolling the cylinders; a hand towel may be substituted. *Norimaki sushi* may be further divided into two categories. One type of roll requires ¼ cup of rice to make, has only one type of filling inside, and is about ¾ inch in diameter; the other, called *futomaki sushi*, requires 1 cup of rice, has several filler ingredients, and is about 2½ inches in diameter.

Ingredients

Sushi rice (page 1905)
Sashimi (usually tuna)
1 cucumber
Toasted sesame seed
1 ounce *kanpyo* (dried gourd shavings)
5 *shiitake* mushrooms
2 eggs (made into an omelette; recipe on page 1906)

Cod roe
Nori (dried seaweed)
Soy sauce
Wasabi (green mustard) mixed with water to form a paste
Dashi (soup stock)
Sugar
Salt

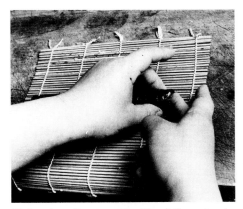

22: Let the roll rest a while. Unroll the mat and use a finger to press in the contents of the roll at both ends.

23: Crosscut the roll in half; then hold the two halves together, and cut six slices of equal thickness, using a sharp knife.

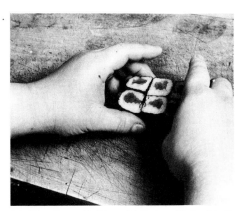

24: The slices of *tekkamaki* (tuna roll) should all be the same height. To achieve this takes a bit of practice.

Small Rolls

Tuna sashimi or raw cucumber with sesame seeds are most often used as the filling in the small rolls. Have a bowl of water near you, and dampen the bamboo mat or towel.

Tekkamaki (tuna rolls): Cut a sheet of *nori* (dried seaweed) in half, and place it on the bamboo mat. Take a scant handful of rice—about ¼ cup—and put it on the left side of the *nori*. Moisten your hands and fingers slightly, and spread the rice over the *nori* (photograph 19). Spread a streak of *wasabi* horizontally across the center of the rice. Place the tuna, which has been cut into small pieces, over the *wasabi* (photograph 20). Place your thumbs beneath the near edge of the mat; gently holding down the contents of the roll with the remaining fingers, turn up the edge and begin to roll toward the far edge (photograph 21). When the edges of the *nori* overlap, squeeze the mat firmly so that the contents adhere to each other in the shape of a roll. Let the roll stand for a few minutes so it will retain its shape after it is cut. Unroll the mat and with your fingers, press in the contents of the roll at the ends (photograph 22). With a sharp knife, cut the roll in half crosswise. Place the two halves together and make three cuts across both halves, forming six slices of equal size (photograph 23). The slices will be neater and the knife will cut more easily if you wipe the blade with a clean, damp cloth after each cut. The completed *tekkamaki* is shown in photograph 24.

Kappamaki (cucumber roll): Peel the cucumber, and cut it in half crosswise and lengthwise, forming quarters. Remove and discard the seeds, and cut the remainder into strips (photograph 25). The basic procedure is the same as for the tuna roll, except that no *wasabi* is used and toasted sesame seeds are sprinkled over the cucumber (photograph 26). If you wish, you may finish the rolls with a decorative cut (photograph 27); the slices are set on their flat ends, angled end uppermost.

25: To make a cucumber roll, cut a peeled, quartered, and seeded cucumber into ¼-inch julienne strips.

26: No *wasabi* paste is used in a cucumber roll; after the cucumber is placed along the rice, it receives a sprinkling of toasted sesame seed.

27: For a decorative effect, you can cut the roll of *kappamaki* into thirds. Then place the three rolls together and make one cut at an angle.

1909

28: To make *futomaki*, a large roll with a mixed filling, spread one cup of sushi rice over a whole sheet of *nori* (dried seaweed). The rice should be about ½ inch deep.

29: The four layers here are *nori* (on top), rice, a hand towel, and (not visible) a bamboo mat. The towel was placed on top of the rice and *nori*; then all were turned over and slid onto the mat.

30: The fillings shown here, from top to bottom are: egg omelette, strips of cucumber, cooked Japanese mushroom, and cod roe. A row of dried gourd stripe remains to be added.

31: Pick up the near end of the towel and roll up the ingredients. Roll tightly and make sure the ends of the *nori* overlap where they meet.

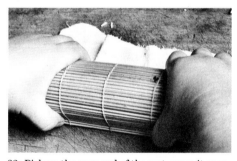

32: Pick up the near end of the mat, wrap it over the towel cylinder, and squeeze gently to firm the consistency of the roll.

Combination Rolls (Futomaki Sushi)

Prepare several of the following fillings beforehand and set them aside until they are needed (these amounts will make six rolls). Peel, quarter, seed, and slice a cucumber into julienne strips as for *kappamaki* (photograph 25, page 1909). EGGS: Cook an omelette, following the recipe on page 1906 but reducing all ingredients by one-third. Cut into ¼-inch-thick slices. DRIED MUSHROOMS: Soak the mushrooms in cold water for 20 minutes, or until soft. Cut off and discard the stems; cut the caps into narrow strips. Put the strips into a small saucepan along with 1 cup of their soaking liquid, 2 tablespoons sugar, 2 tablespoons soy sauce. Bring to a boil and cook until most of the liquid has been absorbed. Allow to cool to room temperature. DRIED GOURD SHAVINGS: Cover with cold water and soak for 30 minutes or until very soft. Bring to a boil; boil for three minutes and drain off the liquid. To this *kanpyo*, add 1 cup *dashi* (soup stock), 2 tablespoons sugar, and 1 teaspoon salt. Bring to a boil; reduce heat and cook, uncovered, until most of the liquid has evaporated. Let cool to room temperature. Place a whole sheet of *nori* (dried seaweed) on the bamboo mat. Spread about 1 cup of rice over the entire sheet (photograph 28). Spread a damp hand towel on the cutting surface; lift up the mat and flip over the *nori* and rice onto the towel, *nori* side up. Place the mat on the cutting surface near the towel and slide the towel, along with the rice and the *nori*, onto the mat. You now have four layers (photograph 29). Arrange one-sixth of each prepared filling across the *nori* (photograph 30). Use the towel and then the mat (photographs 31 and 32) to roll the ingredients into a cylinder. The towel prevents the rice from sticking to the mat. Remove the mat and the towel carefully, and place the roll on the work surface. Wrap a second whole sheet of *nori* around the rice (photograph 33); then place the end of the mat over it and squeeze (photograph 34). Let the roll rest for a minute; then cut into eight equal slices (photograph 35).

33: Place the roll on a second sheet of *nori*. Wrap up the roll in this nori, making sure the ends overlap where they meet.

34: Lay the mat over the cylinder, and apply gentle but firm pressure so the outer sheet of *nori* will adhere to the rice.

35: Press in any of the rice or filling ingredients that may be escaping at the ends. Then slice the roll into eight pieces, each about 1 inch thick.

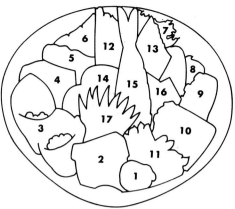

The bowl of *chirashi sushi* contains (1) *wasabi* (Japanese green mustard to be mixed with soy sauce to form a dipping sauce); (2) raw salmon; (3) rolled-up slices of raw squid with salmon roe in the center; (4) raw tuna; (5) raw striped bass; (6) marinated mackerel; (7) seaweed; (8) slices of pickled ginger; (9) raw octopus; (10) fluke; (11) clam; (12, 13) egg omelette; (14) cooked mushrooms; (15) cooked shrimp; (16) pickle slices; and (17) cucumber.

Chirashi sushi, shown above and keyed at right, is a Japanese dish that consists of sweetened, vinegared rice and various toppings such as seafood, eggs, and vegetables.

Kitchen Favorites and Celebrations

Chirashi sushi

When sushi is prepared in a Japanese home, most often it is *chirashi sushi*. This is the easiest to prepare as it consists of various toppings arranged on a bed of vinegared rice. From the toppings below, choose a few that appeal to you.

Ingredients

Sushi rice (recipe on page 1905; about 6 cups will make 6 servings)

Raw fish (page 1903)

Fresh-cooked or canned crabmeat, shrimp, salmon, or mackerel

Eggs (made into an omelette; recipe page 1906)

Wasabi paste (Japanese mustard)

Sweet pickle slices

Shiitake (dried mushrooms); 2 per serving

Nori (dried seaweed)

Fresh seaweed

Pickled ginger

Chirashi sushi is served at room temperature; so prepare the rice and the following toppings, if you are using them, ahead of time to allow them to cool before serving. Boil the crabmeat, shrimp, salmon, or mackerel in plain water; bone, shell, or clean the cooked seafood as necessary for serving. Cook the eggs, following the recipe on page 1906. Soak the *shiitake* (dried mushrooms) in cold water for 20 minutes, or until they are soft. Cut off and discard the stems. Place the whole caps in a small saucepan with 1 cup of their soaking liquid, 2 tablespoons sugar, 2 tablespoons soy sauce. Bring to a boil and cook until most of the liquid has been absorbed. Let cool to room temperature. Just before serving, pile the rice loosely into medium-sized individual bowls. Cover the rice in each bowl with a layer of *nori* which has been torn into bite-sized pieces (use about ½ sheet of *nori* for each bowl). Cut each type of topping into small pieces or thin slices. Place a few pieces of each different topping on top of the *nori* in each bowl. Add thinly sliced pickled ginger and a small ball of *wasabi* paste (mix the powder with water) to each bowl. To serve *chirashi sushi*, place a small individual bowl of soy sauce next to each bowl of sushi. The *wasabi* is mixed with the soy sauce, and the sushi is dipped into the sauce just before it is eaten.

For related crafts and projects, see "Hibachi and Hot-Pot Cookery."

SCRIMSHAW
An American Folk Art

Embued with the spirit of her seafaring New England ancestors, Ruth Edwards creates scrimshaw with contemporary styles and materials (photograph opposite, below). Artist, nature photographer, and avid naturalist, she works in many related crafts, incorporating her designs in silver, fused glass, plastics, and ceramics. Her scrimshaw is sold in Massachusetts shops in Nantucket and Westport, and in Lincoln at the gift shop of the Massachusetts Audubon Society. She is married, has three children, and lives in Westport, where she teaches painting, scrimshaw, and other crafts.

More than a century ago, a folk art was born aboard American whaling ships. Christened scrimshaw (the word comes from British slang, scrimshanker, meaning a time waster), it included objects carved primarily from the teeth and bones of whales, often engraved with scenes and sentiments reflecting the mystique of whaling life. As the whaler drifted in distant seas far from his native New England, sometimes for years at a time, he was accompanied by danger, romance, adventure, and loneliness, all of which find expression in the scrimshaw he carved in his idle hours. It is easy to believe that the same hands that scratched the graphic chase scene on the whale tooth opposite also heaved the ship's lines, furled her sails, or thrust the harpoon home for the kill. And most of the homely objects below, including pie crimpers with fluted wheels, were undoubtedly fashioned for a wife or sweetheart who, as she used them, was reminded of a lover far away.

These antique pieces are artifacts of a bygone era. Today, whaling as a romantic adventure is dead, though whales and other ivory-bearing animals are still being ruthlessly slaughtered. Like many contemporary scrimshanders who are concerned with the preservation of endangered species, I have no intention of replenishing my supply of ivory when it is depleted. For the most part, I work with substitutes for animal ivory. In the bottom photograph opposite are pieces of modern scrimshaw made from a material that is plentiful, inexpensive, usually discarded, and easily obtained—common soup bone. When properly prepared and polished, it can be as lustrous and beautiful as ivory, and the bone shapes themselves lend interest to a surprising number of objects. Other substitutes, such as exotic vegetable ivory and plastics (see Materials, page 1914), are also being used.

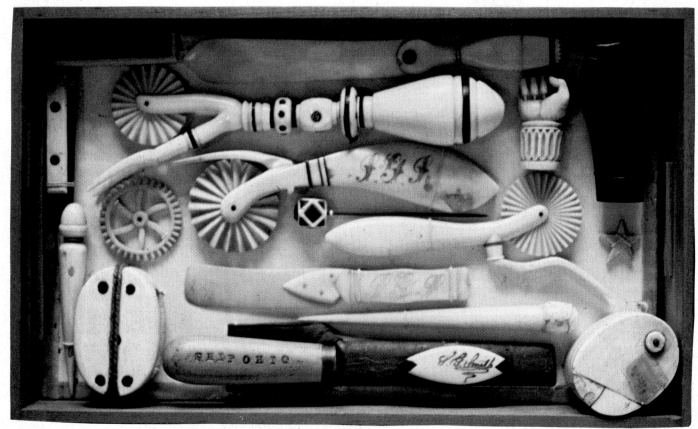

These ivory objects, whimsical and useful, were carved by whalemen more than a century ago. Included are pie crimpers (with fluted wheels), letter openers, bobbins, an awl, hat pin, and a fist.

This chase scene, etched on the tooth of a sperm whale, embodies the spirit and style of antique scrimshaw. In all probability one of the whalemen pictured in the foreground crafted this piece.

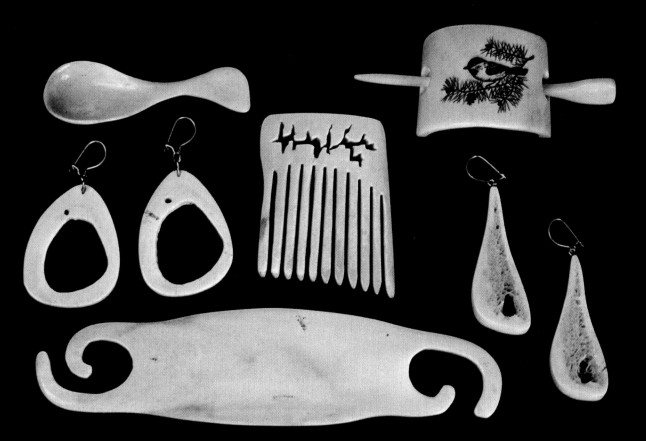

Carved, engraved, and polished to an ivorylike luster, these pieces of contemporary scrimshaw were made from common soup bones, an ecological substitute for ivory from endangered species. Pictured from top are a mustard spoon, hair piece (page 1917), earrings, comb, and shuttle.

Pieces of soup bone that have been sliced, carved, sanded, and polished were used to fashion this striking scrimshaw necklace. The pieces were attached to each other with wire loops glued into holes drilled in the bone.

Raw materials for scrimshaw are shown (above) in various stages of refinement. From left to right they are: soup bone (recommended for ecological reasons), whale's tooth, vegetable ivory nut, elephant ivory, and plastic.

Materials

Ivory is a calcareous material, related to bone but denser and harder. The animal ivories originally used for scrimshaw fall into two categories, tusks and teeth. The teeth of the sperm whale were long cherished for the quality of their ivory, as were the tusks of elephants. Ivory was also obtained from other animals, including the walrus and the hippopotamus. Such ivories differ in their chemical composition and in such characteristics as color, texture, and hardness. Animal ivories can still be purchased, but are becoming scarce and costly. There are restrictions on the interstate transport of whale by-products, and by 1982, all interstate transport of such products will be banned.

Soup Bone

My first choice for an ivory substitute remains leg bones from cattle or sheep salvaged in the kitchen or available from the neighborhood butcher. When correctly cut and polished, such bone has its own unique beauty and is often indistinguishable from some kinds of ivory. One large bone is enough to keep a scrimshander busy carving and engraving for weeks. When you use beef bone, extra preparation is involved (see Craftnotes, opposite); but the result you can achieve with this material makes it worth the effort.

Vegetable Ivory

Ivory nuts are a little-known source of a kind of ivory suitable for making small pieces of jewelry. The ivory nut is the seed of a South American palm tree (*Phytelephas*). A single nut measuring 1 to 2 inches in diameter yields enough ivory for three or four small projects. I know of no ecological reason for not using the ivory nut. It is softer than other ivories and has an interesting grain and a mellow, creamy color. Many of the centers of ivory nuts are hollow or cracked, however, which adds to the design problem of getting the greatest possible use out of the nut.

Synthetics

Plastic ivory substitutes are far softer than bone or ivory and do not compare with them in beauty or durability, but because they are readily available, they serve as good practice material. Several types are available at hobby shops, and at least one manufacturer (Fibre Glass-Evercoat Co., Inc., 6600 Cornell Road, Cincinnati, Ohio 45242) is producing a formula from which you can cast sheets of plastic ivory that can then be cut, polished, and engraved to your liking.

Tools

The whaleman of yesteryear frequently carved whale ivory with a jackknife, then polished it with a gritty piece of dried sharkskin. Today, for anyone who wants to work on only a few pieces, scrimshaw can still be done without power tools. But if you decide to produce many pieces, you will find a few power tools invaluable.

First, you need cutting tools. I use a powered band saw to make the first rough cuts in bone and a jeweler's handsaw for fine work. With a little more work, the rough cuts could be done by hand with a hacksaw. Since bone is very hard, you must use the same kind of blades that you would use to cut metal.

CRAFTNOTES: SCRIMSHAW TECHNIQUES

Preparing beef bone

To prepare a beef bone for scrimshandering, first cut off the raw meat and dig out the soft marrow. (Wild birds, dogs, and cats like bone marrow; so don't throw it away.) A knife blade, spoon handle, or any other convenient tool can be used for removing the marrow. Most of it should come out quite easily. The lacy network of cancellous bone that occurs near a joint can be left and incorporated into the design for your project.

When the bones are clean, add a teaspoonful of alum powder (available at drugstores) and a tablespoonful of baking soda to a quart of water; use more of both if the bone is large. Bring the water to a boil and let the bone cook in this until all fibrous material inside is soft enough to scrape away. Cooking will probably take one and a half to two hours. The smell will be awful; so console yourself with the thought that you are saving money and doing your part to preserve endangered ivory-bearing species. After the bone has been scraped clean, let it dry at least overnight. The bone will whiten as it dries.

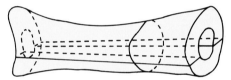

The bone can now be cut with a powered band saw or hacksaw to the rough shape needed. Study the bone carefully before you cut to make sure the piece you get is the one best suited to the project in mind. In the drawing above, some possible cut lines are indicated.

To refine the rough shape, you can use hand files (as shown above), letting the convex side conform with the inner contours and using the flat side on the outer

edges (above). The surface must then be smoothed, starting with coarse sandpaper and working down to finer grades.

Using a powered belt sander (above), start with 60-grit sandpaper and work down in stages to a very fine 320- or 400-grit paper. The last two sandings are done either by hand using wet-and-dry sandpaper, or with a wheel you can make yourself as follows: Cover the buffing edge of a small, stitched buffing wheel (about 3-inch diameter) with glue; then roll the edge in No. 120 silicon carbide grit (sold for rock tumblers). After the glue dries, attach the buffer to a powered wheel for the final sanding.

To buff by hand, put a rag on your work surface and sprinkle it with scouring powder. Rub the bone into the powder for the final sanding; then apply jeweler's rouge and buff with a clean, soft cloth.

Paraffin treatment

If you are planning to engrave the finished piece, stop at the fine-sanding stage when the surface has a frosted finish. Since bone is more porous than ivory, it cannot be engraved successfully without a paraffin treatment that fills the pores and prevents the ink and dyes from bleeding. In a double boiler, melt enough paraffin to cover the bone. (You can improvise a double boiler with a tin can inside a saucepan of boiling water, but be very careful. Paraffin is flammable; so it should never be melted directly over a burner.)

Immerse the sanded bone in the melted paraffin for about five minutes,

just long enough to heat the bone thoroughly so the paraffin will be absorbed into the pores. You do not want a paraffin coat on the outer surface; so when you take the bone from the pan, scrape off excess paraffin. Let the bone cool for about ten minutes; then it is ready for polishing.

Polishing

If you are polishing on a powered buffer, use an unstitched muslin buffing wheel. (Mine is about 8 inches in diameter.) If yours is stitched, rip out the stitches. An unstitched buff is used because it is self-cooling; hence the bone or ivory is less likely to overheat. Use either bobbing compounds or tripoli (both are metal polishing compounds sold by jewelry supply houses and hobby shops).

These come in solid bars that need only to be touched momentarily to the revolving buffing wheel (above) before the bone is buffed. Use white diamond polish or jeweler's rouge for the final polish.

If you have done the previous work carefully, creating an ever finer sanded surface, then buffing takes only a few minutes.

If you are using plastic or ivory nut, the cutting, carving, and polishing processes are much the same, except that you can skip the tedious cleaning process and the paraffin immersion.

In all cases, engraving is done after the final shaping, sanding, and polishing. When the engraving is finished, you can give the scrimshaw object a quick touchup polish on the buffing wheel (above) or with a cloth.

CRAFTNOTES: JEWELRY FINDINGS

Findings are the various types of metal hardware used for attaching and connecting in the assembly of jewelry. Findings include connecting rings that can be opened and closed; chains; earwires, screw backs and clips for earrings; pin backs; tie clips; and cuff-link backs. Bone scrimshaw can be easily drilled to receive rings, then hung on chains to make pendants or earrings.

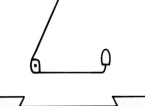

Pin backs, clips, and the like must be glued to the bone. Place the pin slightly above center on the back of the piece and mark the spot with a pencil. To insure a strong bond, dig out some of the bone so the pin back will fit into a groove (as shown above). The ideal tool for this is a powered cone-shaped burr that makes a wider cut at the bottom of the groove than at the top. But an unpowered carbide-tipped graver (see text) will also do the job. Fill the groove with a fast-setting epoxy cement, insert the pin back, and cover the flat bar with more cement. When the epoxy is dry, there is little chance that the pin will loosen.

Special findings, like the bracelet pictured above, often require precisely precut pieces to fit the small frames. These scrimshaw ovals are held in place by a bezel formed over the edge with a burnisher (just as a gemstone is set) or prongs that are tightened with jeweler's needle-nosed pliers.

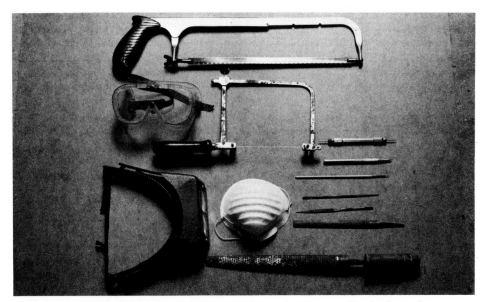

1: Hand tools used for scrimshandering include saws for rough cuts, protective plastic goggles, protective mask for nose and mouth, magnifying glasses, engraving tools, and a half-round rasp.

For shaping the bone, I use a small power drill on a flexible shaft, similar to the kind a dentist uses. Such tools are available under a variety of brand names and cost from $25 to $100. A wide variety of cutting burrs of different shapes facilitates work on small objects so I can get just the contours I need. I do polishing with a powered belt sander and buffing wheel. With patience and energy, however, the same carving and polishing steps could be accomplished with files, hand sanding, and hand buffing.

If you work with power tools, always keep in mind that they are dangerous; handle them with the greatest of care. It is especially important to take every possible precaution when you are working on a small item that could be ripped from your hand and thrown back at you. If you use power tools for cutting, grinding, sanding, or buffing, it is essential that you invest a few dollars in a mask to cover your nose and mouth and in a pair of safety goggles. When bone is ground and sawed with power tools, it produces a very fine dust irritating to eyes, nose, and lungs. Polishing compounds, too, have a wax base that can be injurious to eyes and lungs (see Craftnotes, page 1915).

For engraving pictures in bone or plastic—a major part of most scrimshaw projects—the ideal tool to use is a graver tipped with silicon carbide (photograph 6, page 1918), available in some hardware stores and many hobby, art, and craft supply houses. You can, of course, use anything with a rigid point that will cut bone. A friend of mine does scrimshaw engraving with sharpened worn-out dentist picks. But since the carbide graver costs only a few dollars, is not hard to find, and does a superior job, anything cruder seems a waste to me.

Your decision on what power tools to buy, if any, will depend on how much money you care to invest, how much time and patience you have for any single piece, and whether or not you can improvise with tools already in your workshop. In scrimshaw, as with so many crafts, there is a premium on inventiveness, and a scrimshander's choice of tools is likely to be as individualistic as his finished products.

There is also a special sort of individualism attached to working with a piece of bone or an odd-shaped ivory nut. Once you have cleaned and boiled a soup bone, for example (see Craftnotes, page 1915), don't just start hacking away at it. Study it from all angles. Notice how it twists and turns and varies in thickness, where it widens and contains a lacy, fibrous network near the joints. In every specimen, you will find naturally interesting shapes that can be released through cutting and carving. One bone might be best suited for a long, straight spoon, while another should be turned into a tiny ladle instead. For this reason, do not try to copy exactly any piece pictured here. They are meant to be guides and suggestions. You will be working with different bones, whose unique shapes will be reflected, along with your own perception, in your finished objects.

Carving and Molding
Bone hair piece

$ ● ♣ ♨

The shape of the hair piece pictured at right follows the natural curve of the bone from which it was cut, and the material gives it a rich, mellow, ivorylike luster. Prepare, cut, shape, and polish a bone as described in the Craftnotes (page 1915). If you intend to engrave a design on it, or if you think you might, follow the directions for immersing the bone in paraffin. Using a hand file or powered cutting burrs, shape the outside first, aiming to get the entire piece down to the same thickness, about 3/16-1/4 inch. Use a half-round rasp to do the rough shaping of the inside. If you are using a belt sander on this or any other piece, touch the bone to the sander for only a few seconds at a time, checking frequently to make sure you are not removing too much from any one place. Smooth both inner and outer surfaces with fine sandpaper, polish, then drill the holes for the pin with a power or hand drill. Make the pin from another slice of bone, carving and polishing it the same way. A pin made of ebony or some other dark wood could also be used and would provide an attractive contrast. Whether the pin is straight or slightly curved depends on your personal taste as well as the material you choose.

Once the hair piece and pin are shaped, sanded, and polished, your work can stop, or you can proceed to engrave it.

Engraving on Bone

To engrave your hair piece, you can start by tracing the chickadee design shown (Figure A) or by creating another design (perhaps a monogram) of your own choice. First sketch a large, detailed design as a guide; then redraw the outline the actual size it will be in the finished engraving—drawing on tracing paper or frosted acetate. The latter is more durable, and I recommend it if you will use your design more than once.

With your pattern ready, brush black india ink over the polished bone surface where you plan to engrave the design (photograph 3). When the ink is dry, place white carbon paper, chalk side down, over the inked surface. Center your pattern over the white carbon paper where you want the design to appear. Using an empty ball-point pen or a rounded stylus, trace over the lines of your design (photograph 4). The result will be a crude white line on the surface of the black ink, roughly outlining your subject and giving the correct size and proportion. Remove the carbon and tracing paper. Using a stylus with a sharp point, lightly scratch over the white carbon lines (photograph 5), refining the design. You are not yet engraving, but only scratching a pattern on the bone through the ink. Once this is done, rub off the white carbon line with your finger, leaving the fine white scratched lines showing on a black field. At this point you can decide if you like the design, or if not, change it by scratching directly on the ink with your stylus. Only when the design does please you are you ready to engrave over the white lines. These lines, of course, will be black on the finished piece.

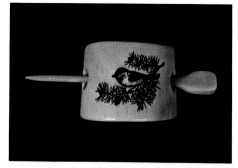

A hair piece engraved with a chickadee design follows the natural curve of the bone from which it was cut (photograph 2). The simplicity of this design makes it a good starting project for first-time scrimshanders.

A
Figure A: Place a piece of tracing paper or acetate over this design, trace it, then transfer it to a bone surface as shown in photographs 3 and 4.

2: Carving and sanding reduced the thickness of the bone piece at left to a uniform thickness of approximately ¼ inch, suitable for the hair piece.

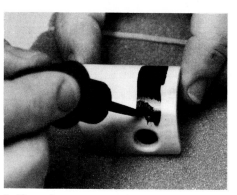

3: If you plan to engrave a design in black on white, first brush the polished surface of the bone with black india ink. Let the ink dry, then put carbon paper and the tracing over the bone.

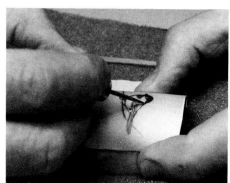

4: Hold the tracing over a piece of white carbon paper on top of the black inked surface. With a rounded tool like a stylus (not a graver), trace lightly over all lines in the design.

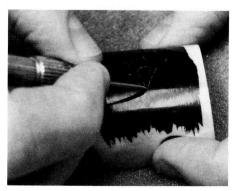

5: With a sharp point, scratch lightly over the white carbon lines, cutting through the ink but barely into the bone. The actual deep engraving of these lines is still to come.

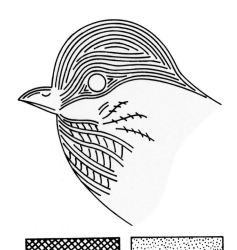

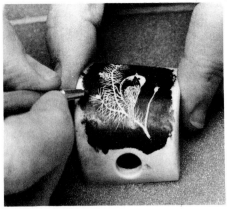

B

Figure B: Shading techniques for drawings or engravings from top to bottom are contoured parallel lines, cross-hatching (left) and stippling.

Using a carbide-tipped engraving tool, go over all the lines, pressing hard enough to cut into the bone (photograph 6). When you work on plastic, you will find it is much softer; vegetable ivory is only a little softer than bone. No one can tell you exactly how hard you should press. You will have to find that out by trial and error. Generally, the harder you press, the deeper and broader you will make the final groove, and thus, the darker it will appear on the finished piece. Experiment by pressing lightly at first; then go back over the lines as necessary to make them deeper and thus darker.

I find a magnifying glass is essential when I am engraving, since the fine lines are sometimes hard to see with the naked eye, and it is necessary to get the graver point into the same groove to deepen it.

Shading

In addition to engraving outlines, you will want to shade whole areas, which calls for other techniques. There are three basic means of shading used in both engraving and drawing, as illustrated in Figure B. The easiest (and least attractive) is cross-hatching—making a series of crossed diagonal lines which, when done with the engraving tool, cut away most of the polished bone surface. The closer the lines are to one another, the blacker an area will look when the grooves are filled with ink. The method I prefer is to engrave parallel lines, following the natural contours of the subject matter. This was done on the chickadee's head. Again, the closer the lines are to one another, the blacker the area will appear. A third method, calling for more painstaking effort, is called stippling; dots are used to create varying degrees of shading. The larger and the closer together you make the dots, the darker the shading will be. I reserve stippling for areas requiring very delicate shading.

Inking

When you have engraved all of the major lines and areas of the design, brush india ink over the entire surface once more and let it dry (photograph 7). Then, with the folded edge of a piece of lightweight cardboard, rub off the ink (photograph 8). All of the ink will easily come off the polished surface except that in the lines and areas you have engraved, leaving a black image on the white bone surface.

It may turn out just as you want it. If not, you are free to make further refinements. Lines can be engraved more deeply, then reinked and wiped. More detail can be added the same way. Check your progress as you work by repeatedly reinking and wiping.

If you make a drastic mistake while you are engraving, all is not lost. But to erase an etched line, you will have to file and sand away that groove; then polish the area again. If the groove is deep and you are working on bone, you may have to repeat the paraffin treatment to make sure that the new surface will take ink without bleeding (see Craftnotes, page 1915).

When you are satisfied with the engraving, lightly touch the surface to the buffing wheel, or buff by hand with a clean cloth, to bring up a final luster.

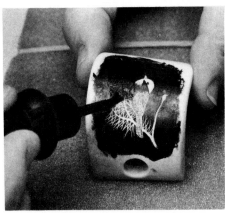

6: Using a carbide-tipped graver, deeply engrave all lightly scratched lines into the bone. A good light and a magnifying glass are helpful when you work on such a small scale.

7: Paint over all the engraved lines with another coat of black india ink. This fills all the engraved lines and etched areas, producing a solid black surface. Allow to dry.

8: When the second coat of ink has dried, wipe the entire surface with the folded edge of a piece of cardboard. This results in the black-on-white lines that appear in the finished piece.

Carving and Molding
Engraving in color

Color-engraved scrimshaw is created by applying pigment or dye instead of india ink to engraved lines. Although the piece above was done on an old slice of whale ivory, the technique is equally applicable to bone or plastic. The pin above is shown enlarged more than twice actual size.

The scrimshaw engraving process is always more or less the same; so the instructions given for the black-and-white hair piece (page 1917) may be applied generally to color engraving on bone or other scrimshaw material. However, the application of color is a bit more complicated; so I recommend that you practice on a few black-and-white projects before attempting it.

When you are ready to try color, prepare the surface to be engraved as described in the Craftnotes, page 1915. The piece of scrimshaw you work on can be anything that pleases you—a spoon, a pendant, or earrings, perhaps. The piece pictured above became a pin. Prepare the design exactly as you would for a black-and-white engraving, drawing your subject (or trace the hummingbird outlined in Figure C) on tracing paper or acetate.

However, this time do not ink the bone surface; leave it white and use regular carbon paper or graphite transfer paper to apply the design. Place the transfer paper where you want the design; then place the design over it. Using an empty ball-point pen or rounded stylus, transfer the design to the bone surface. This will give you crude lines far wider than you want. Use a sharp-pointed stylus to scratch the design lightly onto the bone, refining the crude lines (photograph 9). Then eliminate the carbon by wiping the surface with your finger. At this point, the finely scratched lines will be almost invisible since they are not filled with ink. To see them you must work under a good light and use a magnifying glass. If you tilt the scratched surface slightly under the light, the lines will pick up enough light to become visible.

Next, using the carbide-tip graver, deeply engrave the lines that will be black, and ink them as described for the hair piece (page 1918), rubbing the ink off when it is dry with a folded piece of lightweight cardboard (photograph 8).

Then deeply engrave any lines (not solid areas) that are to be colored. I have tried many coloring agents, and I feel that the best by far is an aniline dye. Unlike ordinary water colors or other pigments, such as colored inks, aniline dyes do not fade when they are exposed to the sun. However, they are damaged by water; so don't wash your painstakingly dyed scrimshaw or wear it while swimming or in the shower. Aniline dyes can be purchased as primary colors, which may be mixed but not diluted. To increase the intensity of a color, use several applications.

C
Figure C: after tracing this hummingbird and flower, transfer it to a polished bone surface by using carbon or gray transfer paper. Do not ink the surface as was done for black-and-white engraving.

9: Scratch over the light tracing lines with a sharp point; then deeply engrave the scratched lines with a carbide-tipped graver (page 1918).

10: All lines or areas that will be black are colored first with india ink applied with a fine brush. Wipe off any excess ink with a folded piece of cardboard as shown in photograph 8.

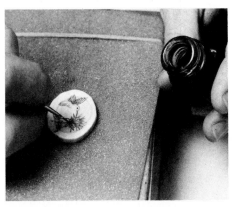

11: Using aniline dyes, apply color to all engraved lines with a tiny brush, trying not to let the dye slip onto adjacent areas. If it does, you can remove it when you are preparing the image to receive areas of solid color.

12: With a carbide-tipped graver, prepare solid areas for coloring by removing all the polished surface there. You can use any of the shading techniques shown in Figure B, page 1918.

13: Finish your colorful scrimshaw, steadyhanded as you go, by painting solid areas with dye. To deepen the color, apply several coats of dye, letting each coat dry before applying the next.

The color must be applied with a very fine paintbrush only to the engraved line (photograph 11), not slopped on the way it is done with india ink in a black-and-white engraving. Put it on very carefully. This requires a steady hand; there is little room for error. (But don't be tempted to dye or paint a scrimshaw picture without first engraving the lines; it will rub off after a little wear, or buff off when you try to give the piece a final polish.)

When you apply color to broad areas, the entire polished surface to be colored must be scratched away to accept the dye. If you crosshatch, stipple, or engrave parallel lines (photographs 12 and 13), you must also scratch the polish from the top of any ridges that remain before you apply dye to the area where you want a solid color. (This process will also remove any dye that overflowed the engraved lines.) Where two areas of solid color meet, the engraving lines should be parallel to keep the dyes from intermingling.

When you are working on such a small scale, you have very little margin for error. Each line must be quite precise. A tiny mistake in drawing a beak, for example, could turn your chickadee into a cardinal.

For related entries, see "Linoleum and Woodcuts," "Sculpture," and "Wood Carving."

Mushrooms and flowers grow, birds and butterflies perch, ducks and swordfish glide on Ruth Edwards' finely wrought scrimshaw jewelry. Pendants, pins, earrings, rings, tie tacks, and thimbles are all subjects for the modern scrimshander's art. Some of the articles above were carved in ivory, but all could be made of bone or plastic.